Mindfully Green

MINDFULLY GREEN

A Personal and Spiritual Guide
to Whole Earth Thinking

Stephanie Kaza

Shambhala
Boston & London
2008

For my mother, who gave me life

Shambhala Publications, Inc.
Horticultural Hall
300 Massachusetts Avenue
Boston, Massachusetts 02115
www.shambhala.com

9 8 7 6 5 4 3 2 1

First Edition
Printed in Canada

∞ This edition is printed on acid-free paper that meets the
American National Standards Institute z39.48 Standard.
♻ This book was printed on 100% postconsumer recycled paper.
For more information please visit us at www.shambhala.com.

Distributed in the United States by Random House, Inc.,
and in Canada by Random House of Canada Ltd

Interior design and composition: Greta D. Sibley & Associates

Library of Congress Cataloging-in-Publication Data
Kaza, Stephanie.
Mindfully green: a personal and spiritual guide to whole earth thinking /
Stephanie Kaza.—1st ed.
p. cm.
Includes bibliographical references.
ISBN 978-1-59030-583-6 (pbk.: alk. paper)
1. Environmentalism—Religious aspects—Buddhism, [Christianity, etc.]
2. Environmental degradation—Religious aspects—Buddhism,
[Christianity, etc.] 3. Human ecology—Religious aspects. I. Title.
GE40.K39 2008
333.72—dc22
2008017289

Contents

PART THREE

ACTING ON GREEN VALUES

Acknowledgments

GRATITUDE FIRST TO MY TEACHERS ON THE PATH; their guiding influence informs this book on every page. I am particularly indebted to Robert Aiken, Thich Nhat Hanh, Joanna Macy, and Gary Snyder for their green wisdom and full hearts. Thanks also to my students and colleagues at University of Vermont who share my passion for this work. May we continue to inspire and encourage each other's creativity as we think hard about what lies ahead.

A special thanks to writing friends Christian McEwen and Patricia J. Anderson, who read earlier drafts of the manuscript with attention and encouragement. Thanks also to my editor, Jennifer Brown, who coaxed the book along to the finish line. Finally, my deepest gratitude to Davis for his endless love and kind support.

Introduction

EVERY SPRING I realize just how lucky I am to be working with people on what I love most—our beautiful world. Why spring? Spring is the season of student achievement, when graduate students and seniors present their bright ideas to the wider community. I get to hear about green maps, carbon planning, smart growth, permaculture, and other hot trends in sustainability. These students give me hope for our world; they are jumping right in to take up the important work of whole earth thinking. Like so many of us, they want to help make the world a better place. This bright energy is exactly what we need today to lift our spirits and encourage our efforts.

At times it can seem like we are making little progress on environmental problems. Over and over I hear these questions: *What can one person do? What should I do?* My answers have come a long way from the early eco-enthusiasm of the 1960s. We felt sure we could save everything if people only knew how much was at stake. Today we face environmental concerns with more awareness, recognizing the political, economic, and social constraints that limit our actions. The more we understand ecosystem complexities and human inequities, the more we realize how much effort it will take to turn the ship toward a sustainable future. Truthfully we can't even begin to realize how much effort it will take. In the last few years there has been a deluge of books on the market and internet websites offering "easy steps" to being green. People everywhere are wanting to do the right thing; there is a hunger for information and guidance. Most often the focus at this first stage of response is personal: *What can I do to create a green lifestyle? How can I live in a more eco-friendly manner?* The guidebooks point out ways to save energy, make wise food choices, and consider green products. These are important steps in the right direction; they offer a way to begin living with the earth's health in mind. But we will need to take this conversation much further if we are to truly address the state of the world today.

This book is a contribution to that conversation, an opportunity to face into the harder questions. Lifestyle change is only part of the path to green living; we also need to spend some time *thinking* about our actions. What are the ethics and values behind our choices? How do we find the emotional and spiritual resolve to keep going under the multitude of challenges? Who can we turn to for green wisdom in these difficult times? What most needs our attention? These are crucial questions that can help shape our actions in a thoughtful way.

As I have listened to students and spoken to audiences around the country, I have been struck by what could be called "green zeal," an almost fervent sense of engagement with environmental concerns. People feel passionately about protecting rain forests and whales; they want everyone to know that polar bears and penguins are threatened. Behind the passion is a deeply felt need to do something right, to find a way to correct our past environmental errors. Almost no point on the globe is free of human influence now; we have left our mark in virtually all the world's ecosystems. People today feel the sorrow of these thoughtless actions in the past—the once-expansive forests so diminished, the native peoples decimated. There is a great well of shame and grief wanting relief from the painful consequences of our own shortsighted actions. This manifests as a need for healing, for making life changes that will take us in a kinder direction, one that can sustain our own lives as well as the rest of life on earth.

Our anxiety over an uncertain future has become particularly acute with the new understanding that climate change will affect us all. We have the sense that global support systems are lurching out of control, that things have gone too far, that we may already be in serious danger. Climate advocates are urging government leaders to invest in a green vision for a more hopeful future. Businesses are making energy and waste audits to cut costs and improve long-term economic viability. Voters are calling for a "green jobs" economy to help us make the shift from fossil fuels to renewable energy. Green zeal is necessary to change our ways quickly, to meet environmental goals that would be impossible without global cooperation.

In the midst of so much greening activity, many people are making significant changes to their lives, taking up what I've come to call the "green practice path." They are changing their lightbulbs, taking the bus, insulating their homes, serving on community boards, and passing along green values to their children. From what I've observed, these efforts are based in much deeper motivation than home improvement. People are thinking deeply about what matters to them and taking their actions seriously. I believe they are bringing their best ethical and spiritual attention to environmental concerns and trying to match their actions to their moral principles.

People come to green practice from many walks of life and are taking initiative in many different arenas. Green zeal is turning up in every corner of the earth. Thousands of people are living their own inspiring stories as they find a way to share their green ethics on behalf of a more peaceful and genuinely happy world. There is no single green path; the path is determined by individual experience, local needs, and personal motivation. The green path is, by and large, a secular practice, open to all who feel the call. It seems to me to reflect what the Dalai Lama calls an "ethics for the new millennium," an ethics built on compassion, restraint, and acceptance of universal responsibility for the well-being of the earth.

If we engage green living in more depth, it becomes an expression of our deepest moral values. The "work" of green living becomes less a chore and more a locus of ethical development. We conserve water not because we *should* be frugal but because we respect the earth's resources. This shift in thinking and understanding can be quite profound. The conversation moves from personal sacrifice to real consideration of the nature of our connection with the earth. When we come to see ourselves as part of the great web of life, in relationship with all beings, we are naturally drawn to respond with compassion.

This book offers one entry point to this way of thinking about the environment. In these pages I've outlined three aspects of the green practice path. Part 1, "Seeking Green Principles," identifies a core set of principles for setting out on the path. This approach is based on an ethical foundation that emphasizes the importance of reducing harm to the earth in order to help life flourish. Once we recognize the environmental impacts caused by human action, we can make a conscious effort to reduce that harm on behalf of the planet. Reducing harm requires that we face the suffering of the world as it is, including the egregious ravaging of ecosystems that degrades them beyond repair. Both these orientations are informed by taking the deep view of systems thinking, a way of seeing that promotes effective problem-solving and respect for differences in viewpoint.

Part 2, "Following the Green Path," offers ways that each of us can strengthen our personal commitment to green practice, moving from novice to what I call a "lifeway." Lifeway practice is based in clear intention, community engagement, and shared wisdom. This shift involves finding the causes that speak to us and developing the resolve to stay committed to the work. But the path is not without obstacles, so we need to work directly with the emotional challenges of doubt, anxiety, anger, and despair as part of the practice. To help along the way, we must find sources of wisdom and inspiration in the form of teachers and friends. These may be wise human elders steeped in the green tradition or beings much older than ourselves—the trees, oceans, and mountains. All of these wisdom resources can help us find our way in a very uncertain world.

Part 3, "Acting on Green Values," the final section of the book, takes up specific arenas for engaging the green practice path. In this section, we consider three broad practice fields that offer multiple opportunities for personal and global action. We first look at how to develop energy awareness, considering how to conserve and maintain energy and exploring why that is necessary in a consuming world. Second, we investigate the nature of desire and examine its multiple allures for today's consumers. In the context of desire, Buddhist teachings are very effective in developing inner discipline that supports the practice of restraint while cultivating the antidote of contentment. Finally, we explore the ways that our capacity for earth-keeping can be greatly improved by investing in peace. These three practice arenas—maintaining energy, managing desire, and coming to peace—can provide a solid spiritual foundation for walking the green practice path and cultivating inner strength for the journey.

This book reflects my own experience with Buddhist teachings in addressing environmental issues. I have found traditional Buddhist wisdom to be practical and down-to-earth as well as being supportive of spiritual practice. The Buddha insisted that students should test the teachings for themselves and see what worked to reduce their suffering and open doorways to understanding. The teachings in this book are offered in that spirit as part of the experiment of the green practice path. I hope you will find something of value in them and can apply their pragmatic advice in your own work on this path, whether you consider yourself a Buddhist or not. As with many of the world religions, the time-tested teachings of Buddhism offer important wisdom that can guide us through the difficult challenges we face today. The Buddhist tradition is particularly rich in its understanding of the interdependence of people and nature, an emphasis reflected in the strong ethical admonition to respect all life and refrain from killing. Buddhism is also very sophisticated in its treatment of desire, the fundamental driver in consumerism. Westerners today seem to be finding Buddhist contemplative practices useful in slowing down the helter-skelter pace of modern electronic life. Such reflective time is almost certainly necessary to make the deep changes required by the global environmental crisis at hand.

The principles and stories in this book arise from my own spiritual commitment to Buddhist practice. I have been a student of Zen Buddhism for most of my life, having benefited from the great flowering of Buddhism in America in the late twentieth century. As I began my academic career, the scholarly field addressing religion and environment was just emerging. Because of my practice background in Buddhism, I was often asked to provide a Buddhist perspective on environmental questions. Much of my writing over the past twenty years has contributed to the field of Buddhist environmental thought. At the same time I have been teaching college students introductory and elective courses in environmental studies, staying up-to-date with the latest issues and approaches to environmental problem-solving. My approach to these concerns is both contemplative and pragmatic.

I have come to my own green practice path as an environmental educator, a professor, a writer, and an advocate for sustainability. Since the first Earth Day in 1970, I have been an environmentalist in one form or another, often as a teacher taking up the job of promoting environmental awareness. My work is deeply satisfying—it is a life-calling, and I am grateful that over these many years I have been able to share my environmental concerns with young people, activists, colleagues, and readers far and wide. I am also grateful for all my colleagues who keep us moving forward. I see this book as yet another opportunity to pass the green spark on to others, especially those who will follow me in this work.

It is my hope that the ideas, tools, and practices presented in this book can be of benefit to anyone passionate about saving the planet. In my own life these principles and practices give me strength to continue this work and share it with others. This book is an exploration of my personal sense of the green path; it is only one view. There are many ways to express and act on our love for the earth, our home. May these ideas be of use and may the merit of this work serve the many beings we live with here on this beautiful and fragile blue pearl.

PART ONE

Seeking Green Principles

1

Reducing Harm

TO GET OUR BEARINGS on the path, it is helpful to have some compass points for orientation. The first three chapters of this book consider principles that provide an ethical foundation and a pragmatic direction for the green path. Foremost of these is the commitment to reduce harm wherever possible. We begin by looking at the nature of environmental harm and exploring choices to reduce that harm. Offering kindness becomes a core practice of non-harming, a way to be with the suffering of the natural world, hard as this may seem. To gain a wisdom perspective on harm and suffering, the third chapter takes up the deep view based on interdependence. With ethical principles and systems thinking to guide us, we can have a certain measure of confidence in setting out on the path.

REDUCING HARM

The Dalai Lama often opens his speeches by saying, "Everyone wants to be happy. No one wants to be unhappy." Stemming from this statement is much of the world's moral and religious philosophy. Another way to put this is, "Everyone wants to be unharmed. No one wants to be harmed." All beings, from baby grasshoppers to giant redwood trees and people the world over, would prefer to be safe, to be free from harm, injury, violence, and suffering, to be allowed to live their lives in peace. Nobody really wants to be hurt, abused, or threatened in any way.

The Christian principle of reducing harm is contained in the Golden Rule: "Do unto others as you would have them do unto you." In 1993 the Parliament of the World's Religions proclaimed this moral code of reciprocity or mutual respect to be the common basis for a global human ethic. For Hindus, this is expressed as the practice of *ahimsa,* or non-harming—that is, taking up the path of not causing harm. In Buddhism, monks and laypeople take vows to "save all sentient beings from suffering." Reducing harm through mutual respect is a central ethical principle in all religious and ethical traditions because it is fundamental to keeping human societies functional and not self-destructive. It is difficult for people and their support systems to thrive if everyone is hurting each other all the time.

This same logic can be extended to human relations with ecological systems. It is difficult for ecosystems to thrive and for people to thrive in them if plants and animals, groundwater, streams, mountains, oceans, and air are constantly under assault. Damaged support systems don't work as effectively as healthy systems. They are less resilient, less capable, and less functional overall. Human beings trying to live in damaged or ailing ecosystems don't do well either. They pick up waterborne disease from polluted streams. They struggle with asthma from poor air quality. They are vulnerable to extreme weather events from climate change.

So what does it mean to reduce harm? How can such a principle work when applied in a practical situation? How would one use such a guideline to be a good ecological citizen? As you would imagine, most environmental questions do not have simple answers. We don't always know when harm is being done, and even when we can see there is harm, we don't always know what the cause is. And further, there may be many reasons why it is difficult to reduce the harm that is happening. Choosing the ethical path of reducing harm turns out to be a complex and demanding practice. But that should not discourage us. Many wisdom traditions have prepared the way for this practice, and we can work with well-proven methods to help us along the path.

DEGREES OF HARM

In any given situation, people try to work out a way to get what they need without causing too many repercussions. We are constantly evaluating trade-offs and potential risks to minimize harm to ourselves as well as others with whom we have ongoing relations. We learn to do this in our family settings as we cope with household stress while keeping our safety intact. We maintain polite protocols to be good neighbors even if we disagree on politics. This balancing act reflects our evolutionary development as social animals; there are many good sociobiological reasons for being well-practiced at evaluating the potential for harm. Those who do this well assure both their own well-being and the well-being of their kin. Since this process of discrimination is already well developed, we can use it to help us on the green practice path. In order to reduce environmental harm, we must be able to identify it and then evaluate our own contribution to that harm.

Everyone has to eat, so this is a good place to practice looking for environmental harm and checking our participation in that harm. By "practice," I mean engaging the questions around harming for a period of time and asking them over and over in different contexts. It is a form of discipline, remembering that this is what you are trying to do, bringing your attention back to the questions with a fresh mind again and again. Practicing with food presents an opportunity for mindfulness because so much of our time is spent in obtaining, preparing, and consuming food. When we stop to consider how much harm is involved in growing or making our food, we can make more informed choices about what we eat and what degrees of harm we will embrace.

Let's explore several ways of evaluating degrees of harm in food. Looking at the broad picture, we can measure the various environmental impacts generated by the growing and processing the major food groups. Fortunately for us, the Union of Concerned Scientists has already done this research, laying down reliable benchmarks based on scientific analysis. These are outlined in their book *The Consumer's Guide to Effective Environmental Choices.*[1]

The authors considered 120 types of environmental impacts and then consolidated this list to six primary concerns: air and water pollution, land use, solid and hazardous waste, and climate change. They then examined U.S. national data for producing all of our food sources—fruits, vegetables, grains, meat. They were able to show which impacts were associated with each type of food production. Their study indicates that meat production is the leading cause of agricultural water pollution. This is because cows and hogs are fattened for slaughter in large feedlots and their manure runs off into the groundwater, polluting nearby streams and lakes. Production of grains and vegetables takes its toll on soil health and habitat biodiversity. So we can use factual data to measure the types and degrees of harming—in the arena of food production and other areas as well.

Another way to evaluate harm is to examine the impacts on individual plants and animals that we choose to consume. Many people are concerned about the treatment of animals in the industrial food system, which causes distress and suffering for the animals. Classic philosophical arguments for vegetarianism point out that animals have awareness and intelligence, that they experience physical and emotional suffering as we do. The infliction of cruelty and suffering—such as clipping hogs' tails, cutting chicks' beaks, or branding the hides of cattle—are standard operations in domestic meat production. Animals experience further anxiety and stress from being crowded in small cages or packed into trucks for long-distance transport. Calves and piglets are often traumatically separated from their mothers before weaning. If you eat meat, you can evaluate which of these types of harming is acceptable to you. If you want to reduce harm to the soil and groundwater as well as to individual animals, you can reduce the amount of meat you eat. The Union of Concerned Scientists strongly recommends cutting back on meat consumption to directly reduce both animal suffering and environmental degradation.

Evaluating harm to plants is more difficult because we don't understand how plants experience harm. We know that poor soil, lack of water, and overharvesting can leave plants weak and nutrient-deficient. But do plants suffer in the same way if their evolutionary integrity is altered through genetic engineering? Does mono-cropping harm plants or soils or both? With the rise of the organic farming movement, green consumers looking to reduce harm choose organic over conventional produce options. They reason that organic plants have been better nourished by the soil and perhaps also more lovingly cared for by the farmer, at least in small-scale operations. Workers on industrial-scale organic farms, however, may not hold such intimate relations with their crops.

Another way to evaluate degree of harm is in terms of the eater, rather than the eaten. Meat-intensive diets have been correlated with high rates of human heart disease and cancers of the digestive tract. Some vegetarians have turned away from meat to protect their health and avoid meat-associated medical risks. Studies now show that hormones used in beef production can affect human reproductive development, causing early puberty and male infertility. The heavy use of antibiotics in conventional meat and dairy operations is a human health concern as well, undercutting the effectiveness of these valuable drugs in treating human infection. Reducing harm to ourselves is a viable and important aspect of reducing environmental impact, reflecting the recognition that we too are part of the environment that is under siege.

We can also consider degrees of harm relative to spiritual well-being. In many world and indigenous religious traditions, abstaining from meat is a common practice in cultural ceremonies or as training in self-discipline. Practicing restraint requires constant vigilance and the tempering of deeply conditioned appetites. Buddhists and Hindus emphasize the merit gained from cumulative acts of compassion in relation to animals. They further believe that a meat-free diet generates a calmer mind, more disposed toward equanimity and patience and therefore less likely to harm others.

In the last few years a new criterion has arisen for evaluating harm: the distance a food has traveled from production to market. The harm, in this case, is to our climate, since long shipping distances contribute significantly to the carbon emissions impact of food products. Farmers' markets across the nation have been promoting "locavore" campaigns, challenging people to eat 10 or 20 percent of their diet from local foods only. Authors Barbara Kingsolver and Gary Nabhan have taken on the experiment of eating 100 percent locally in their Midwest and desert regions, inspiring others with their stories. In this measure, degree of harm reflects the number of food miles associated with a specific food. We can choose to reduce our diet-related greenhouse gas emissions by eating locally and cutting down on food miles.

NO UNNECESSARY HARM

Evaluating harm in these specific ways takes research and self-reflection. In most cases, the information we need to make sound ethical decisions is not available on the food labels. Our choices often must be based on incomplete knowledge and some amount of guesswork. For some people, animal suffering is the most significant harm; others are concerned more with harm to soil and climate. It is not possible to stay up-to-date on every bit of product information in order to reduce harm. The Buddhist poet Gary Snyder offers another approach based broadly on what we might call "whole earth thinking." He speaks of the necessity of eating as an opportunity for spiritual practice, where everyday actions are the manifestation of your personal ethics. The green practice path becomes less a process of changing the foods we eat but of eating with a larger view, transforming our inner orientation to eating. For Snyder, this larger view is "one that can acknowledge the simultaneous pain and the beauty of this complexly interrelated real world."[2] In his wily Zen way, Snyder urges us to face the fact that causing harm is necessary for us to live. There is no harm-free lunch. We all participate in the big story of eating and being eaten. There is no way to escape this fact. If our spiritual goal is to reduce harm in the world, we must ask some hard questions: *What do I actually need? What is my fair share? How do my choices impact the food available to others?*

Questions like these are not meant to be answered quickly or completely. Any single answer is bound to be inadequate. Choosing vegetarianism, for example, is not a final or complete answer to the harm associated with food. Body needs change over time; a colder climate may require you to eat more warming, high-protein foods such as meat. Choosing to eat locally may work well in summer, but do you have the time to can and freeze enough food to get through winter? The point is to ask these hard questions with full attention and see where they lead you, being ethical but also realistic. In Zen this sort of question is called a *koan,* a continually unfolding puzzle that takes more than mental effort to answer. You live with a koan, you wrestle with it, you get stumped by it, you have sudden breakthroughs with it—all with the question burrowing itself into you like an irritating thorn. The path of "committing no unnecessary harm," as Snyder puts it, is riddled with such questions. If you come to answers too quickly, you will have missed the deeper insight hidden in the questions.

As an ethical foundation for the green practice path, finding ways to reduce harm in all aspects of our lives is imperative. We have been considering the fundamental activity of eating as one place to evaluate harm, but we could look at any of our activities and take up the same questions. You could examine your use of water or the disposal of your waste, investigating which lands and waters are affected, which neighborhoods suffer. Then you would wrestle with other questions: *How much water do I need? What is the cost of my waste? Who on the planet is affected by my needs for water and my production of waste?* Keeping a firm focus on reducing harm in all of our activities can provide a strong moral compass for the green practice path. "Compass" is a useful metaphor here, for we can only aim in the right direction and then do the best we can. There are no absolute answers waiting for us; as poet Rainer Maria Rilke has said, we must "learn to love the questions."

Sometimes it can be helpful to raise these questions with other people who are also seeking viable alternatives to causing harm. I think of my colleagues at the Center for Whole Communities who are working hard to craft real-life answers to these questions. Every summer, groups of land conservation professionals, environmental advocates, and community organizers come to Knoll Farm in Vermont for weeklong retreats in "whole thinking." The center is committed to caring for the land and maintaining a working farm on the property. The closely run operation depends on constant input and reflection from the staff. Guests are invited to participate in this reflection across the week through dialogue discussions supported by meditation. The day's schedule begins and ends in silence, providing plenty of space for considering less harmful ways of living.

At the straw-bale bathhouse, retreatants find instructions in minimizing harm by practicing attention to water. The convivial rounded hall was built of mud and straw and decorated with stained glass; its beauty is a testimony to the loving hands that shaped it. Standing by the woodstove and lanterns, you sense that you would not want to cause any harm to the spirit of the place through your own carelessness. Small signs in the restrooms remind people to conserve water, since the solar pump can only move water uphill at the modest rate of one gallon per minute. The showers have been left open to the sky, evoking Gary Snyder's big view of the universe. This, too, contributes to reducing harm through appreciation of our place in the very wide universe.

Whole thinking retreats ask participants to consider how the land is harmed by people and also how people harm each other in the process of being careless about their impact on the environment. The Center for Whole Communities is dedicated to raising challenging questions about diversity and justice in land-protection efforts. Knoll Farm retreat groups purposely include urban gardeners or advocates for environmental justice from culturally and racially diverse backgrounds. These environmental leaders are protecting open spaces and community gardens in urban areas, often with little economic or political support. They are quick to point out the privileges and benefits that come with race, class, or gender status. Not everyone has the same opportunities to make choices to reduce harm. The koan of "no unnecessary harm" must also include the harm to fellow human beings who work as laborers harvesting crops or line workers in the slaughterhouse. How do we understand the harm we consume that is tied up with human sweat?

The underlying curriculum in every aspect of Knoll Farm is this consideration of harm. Teachers encourage retreatants to look closely at these problems in a calm and present way. This is very helpful for sorting out degrees of harm. People are asked to consider these questions, among others: What is the nature of environmental and human harm? How does it impact workers and families? How is the harm manifested? Can it be reduced or moderated? The answers are arrived at collectively, through mutual support in dialogue conversations, with everyone's experience becoming a piece of the whole. The hope is that people will carry this curriculum back to their own lives and let it enliven their work in the world.

The staff at Knoll Farm draw on the teachings of Buddhism and other wisdom streams to invite a deeper sense of personal reflection when considering degrees of harm. In Buddhist spiritual practice, monks work with non-harming by taking vows to uphold specific ethical guidelines to the best of their ability. The first of these formal precepts is stated unequivocally: *do not kill*. It is considered a serious ethical injunction, aimed at protecting life. The other core precepts build on this first command, pointing to the root of Buddhist understanding: all things are related and interdependent. To protect the life of others is to protect your own life. Vietnamese Zen teacher Thich Nhat Hanh has phrased this precept with strong guiding language to help his students with their practice.

> Aware of the suffering caused by the destruction of life, I vow to cultivate compassion and learn ways to protect the lives of people, animals, plants, and minerals. I am determined not to kill, not to let others kill, and not to condone any act of killing in the world, in my thinking, and in my way of life.[3]

The verbs in this passage are important: "vow" means "I commit to giving this my full intention"; "learn ways" means "I still have much to find out about taking care of life." This orientation suggests an openheartedness, a sense of being willing to try hard, given that we don't have all the answers and never will. Thich Nhat Hanh sees the precepts not as a set of rules but rather as an ethical compass providing guidance for our actions. If we take this precept seriously, it becomes clear that "no unnecessary harm" applies not only to all living beings and the earth but also to our own minds and thoughts.

The practice of non-harming, or aiming to reduce harm wherever possible, is not a trivial undertaking. I believe this is a central ethical guideline on the green practice path. In the northern Buddhist tradition, non-harming is known as the great vow, the bodhisattva vow. A bodhisattva is a "heroic benefactor" and guide, an archetype of liberating energy, a figure who embodies tremendous

motivation for helping others.[4] Bodhisattvas are radiant, enlightening beings that exist in myriad forms, appearing as needed in any
given situation. The bodhisattva vow is the pledge to reduce suffering
and to care for all beings in whatever way possible. The full scope of
bodhisattva practice includes but also extends broadly beyond environmental concerns to address harming in all its manifestations.
Making such a pledge is a statement of intention; the pledge itself
helps to strengthen that intention.

An "ecosattva" is one form of bodhisattva—someone who cares
deeply about all beings and the health of the planet and is willing to
take action after action to help all beings thrive. This word was first
coined by Buddhist activists in northern California engaged in forest
protection actions. One of the most beloved bodhisattvas in the Buddhist tradition, Jizo, embodies this definition of an ecosattva. Jizo is
known as a protector of vulnerable children and travelers, willing to
go to the ends of the world to help those who are suffering. His name
means "earth storehouse" or "earth womb." Sometimes called the
"earth mother" bodhisattva, Jizo's vow is filled with tenderness and
compassion. He makes it seem possible to continue to engage these
tough questions in everyday real life. We can look to ecosattvas in real
life for inspiration to keep going with the endless work before us.

OFFERING KINDNESS

The Dalai Lama often tells people, "I am a simple monk, that is all. I
only wish to practice kindness." Although he holds the highest degrees in Tibetan Buddhist philosophy and is recognized as a world
religious leader, he insists his central practice is to offer kindness to
himself and to others. This is really the heart of non-harming. Kindness is the balm for alleviating suffering; offering kindness is a way of
practicing non-harming. Here, surely, is something that applies in
all situations of environmental concern. How can we find a way to

offer kindness that will reduce the suffering of trees or birds or people on the land? How can kindness help mitigate conflicts between opposing parties? How can the practice of kindness make life more sustainable for those committed to environmental work?

Reducing harm is not something that is done only in situations "out there." It is internal work, too, a practice in reducing harm to body and mind. This precious self, the one who wants to be a good eco-neighbor on this planet, the one who struggles with these dilemmas, he or she, too, is in need of kindness. Practicing kindness to yourself is essential in taking up the path of non-harming. It will not be possible to solve all of the earth's environmental problems in one lifetime. If you choose to take up the green path, you must settle in for the long haul and rest in the practice itself. A strong wish for the well-being of others can then be grounded and reinforced in a strong wish for your own well-being. This is not really being selfish, it is being practical. The less energy that is bound up in negative thought patterns or personal distress, the more energy is available for serving others. The greater the care you give yourself, the more you will be able to take on challenges for others. The more clear and calm your mind, the more you will be able to see how to act ethically in a given situation.

Environmental work is not an easy path. It brings up all our concerns for the very flourishing of life on this planet. Reducing harm, taking up the path of not killing—this is a place to begin, a life practice that is espoused by all the world's great philosophical and religious traditions. It is wise but practical, too. And no one is left out. Offering up the great bodhisattva vow of intention, we can face fearlessly into each environmental concern, looking for ways to offer kindness and sooth suffering. The practice itself is about staying present, one action at a time, always asking, What is the kind thing to do now?

2

Being with the Suffering

WITH ALL OUR BEST EFFORTS, it will still be impossible to eliminate all of the harm being done to the world. The scale of environmental suffering is too widespread and too deeply entrenched. Many of today's predicaments were set in motion long before our time. Many situations are simply out of our control. While we can do our best to reduce the harm associated with our own actions, we are limited in how much we can reduce the extensive harm caused by others. Even if we convert our homes to solar energy, it will be a long time before the coal-mining scars are healed. Even if we stop eating meat, factory farms will continue to harm the environment, and animals will still be slaughtered for human use. How do we cope with this understanding? How do we respond to the large-scale harm being done to the earth? In this chapter we look at how to witness the suffering of the earth, trace the causes of suffering, and cultivate a compassionate heart on the green practice path.

THREATS TO LIFE

Today we look around the world and there is no shortage of environmental suffering. Strip-mining for coal now destroys whole mountains in West Virginia, filling valley streams with sludge and people's homes with toxic waste. Millions of used computers are shipped to China, where valuable parts are stripped out as people breathe acid fumes; useless material is dumped in nearby waterways. In the middle of the Pacific Ocean a floating waste dump the size of Texas collects billions of pieces of plastic debris—false "food" that attracts animals from up and down the ocean food chain. When we see or hear of this scale of suffering we have a very natural response: *Oh no! This is not good!* We sense the harm as a threat to life and the well-being of the world. We feel compelled to block the threat for our own safety or somehow reduce its impact. This response is very much at the root of the modern environmental movement.

The environmental activism of the 1960s arose out of a collective response to witnessing suffering and understanding the greater threats to all life on earth. We were all ecologically naïve then, uninformed about the complicated biogeophysical relations that sustain life in all the world's eco-regions. The earth seemed to absorb our human insults and continue to support life, as far as we could tell. We thought, *Plow the soil into farmland and it will grow food. Cut the forest down and seedlings will sprout to form a new forest.* In the United States, with all its spacious lands and abundant waters, a frontier mentality reigned right into the twentieth century. No matter what we did, most people were sure there would always be plenty to go around.

While I was in college in the 1960s, I thought I would try to ride my bike to Lake Erie. I had come to Oberlin College from western Oregon and really had no idea what the Great Lakes were. I pedaled with some anticipation through the cornfields of northern Ohio, enjoying the fresh air and local apple stands. But when I finally arrived at the shore, I was horrified. Hundreds, maybe thousands of dead fish lined the edge of the water. As far as I could see were piles after piles of stinky fish. What were they doing there? Why were they dead? I felt sick to my stomach and angry all at once. What could possibly have caused such an upheaval of death in this lake? I knew that something was very wrong here, but I did not know what to do or who to tell about it. My innocent bike ride turned into an ecological epiphany.

That vivid image was soon upstaged by newspaper photos of the Cuyahoga River on fire. How could a river burn? Were things that bad? I signed up for the first ecology course offered at Oberlin; maybe this new science would explain what was going on. Ecologists were documenting the complex and highly evolved patterns of biological relations in land and water systems, throwing out many previous assumptions about the natural world. I found out that I was not the only one who was concerned about impacts on the environment. Senior scientists were sounding the alarm, speaking out on population growth, air pollution, the increasing pressures on earth systems. These concerns built on the fears unleashed by the shocking destruction of World War II. We now knew that atomic bombs could destroy all life on earth. We now knew that people could carry out unspeakable atrocities such as Auschwitz. Innocence around the world was shaken by these extremes, throwing people off once-solid moorings, exposing the true human capacity for destruction. No one said anything about the impact on non-human life, but there it was: we could destroy that too. Was the human race a scourge on the earth?

The strong stirrings of concern for the environment in the 1960s were galvanized by this sense of threat. As each new loss or harm was exposed, the scale of urgency seemed to multiply. The prosperity of postwar times spurred energy and transportation development and increased production of consumer goods. As demand for resources escalated, ecosystems were under assault everywhere, especially in the western United States. The Sierra Club launched a campaign to save the stark redstone beauty of the Southwest from hydroelectric energy projects. "Save Glen Canyon" became the rallying cry in an effort to hold back the engines of the industrial economy. Despite extensive promotion and political lobbying, environmentalists failed to stop the damming of the canyon. To people's great sorrow, the exquisitely sculpted walls of Glen Canyon were buried under millions of tons of water.

Around the same time, an oil platform suffered a blowout off the southern coast of California, and the buildup of pressure caused two hundred thousand gallons of crude oil to leak from the ocean floor. It took eleven days to fix the break; four thousand seabirds died from oil clogging their feathers. Beaches were ruined with the black tar that washed up for miles north and south of Santa Barbara. Newspaper photos showed dedicated volunteers carrying hopelessly soiled seabirds to rescue centers. President Richard Nixon observed that the Santa Barbara incident had "touched the conscience of the American people."

The mounting threats to the natural world seemed to call forth a spiritual urgency for those who feared the whole ecological foundation of life was at serious risk. It was our human duty to correct the errors of our ignorance; many saw this as our shared ethical responsibility. As the war raged in Vietnam and feminists called for gender justice, environmental issues took on a depth of ethical concern that reflected the social upheaval of the times. Spurred by public outcry, the United States Congress passed law after law in remarkable time, protecting endangered species, marine mammals, clean water, and fisheries.

But still the stories continued, making it clearer than ever that human life and health were threatened by environmental abuse. With the 1978 toxics leak at Love Canal, near Niagara Falls, New York, and the Three Mile Island nuclear accident near Harrisburg, Pennsylvania, less than a year later, ordinary people began to realize: *this could happen to me*. Although the twenty-five thousand people within five miles of the partial reactor meltdown were spared extreme harm, the accident set off shock waves in people's imaginations. We could all see that any nuclear reactor was vulnerable to accident and that anyone living near a hazardous dump site, oil refinery, industrial factory, or landfill was personally at risk from environmental disasters just waiting to happen.

How does an organism respond to the threat of harm? Animals of all kinds are hardwired with a lifesaving response system of fight or flight. We survive a threat by running away to safety or by fighting the attacker and defending ourselves. These strategies have evolved over thousands of years of living with fires, floods, and predators. Both responses, however, are completely inadequate in the face of widespread environmental suffering. We have seen the photos from space of the "blue pearl," our small planet against the huge darkness. We can't really run away; there is only this one earth and its very thin, fragile layer of life. Fighting the attacker is tangled up with politics, business, the economic health of the nation—a very complex beast to attack. With these basic "fight or flight" impulses so clearly inadequate, people concerned about the environment have turned to higher orders of thinking. The ethical call is unavoidable. In the first decade of the twenty-first century, with climate change high on the global political agenda, that call is recognized by more people around the world than ever. Even if we don't know exactly what to do, we must turn to face what is happening and find a way to respond.

WITNESSING SUFFERING

Much of our ignorance about ecological degradation is the result of not seeing, not smelling, not tasting, not hearing, and not feeling the deeper impacts of environmental suffering. We are too busy or perhaps too afraid to pay attention to what is going on. It is easy to see suffering when it has gone to extreme levels—it's hard not to notice a burning river. But we need to be able to see the *causes* of these environmental disasters, to see the suffering as it is developing. Environmental suffering is the combined suffering of individuals and the systems they are part of and that support their lives. Gardeners are well aware of this: if you see a plant with yellow leaves, you check the soil to see which nutrients are missing. When a plant is ailing, its failure to thrive signifies a weakness in the system that supports it. If the blossoms fall without setting fruit, you check for interfering pests. Learning to make the connections between individuals and systemic suffering is part of becoming a useful witness. This is one of the most basic practices on the green path: simply seeing what is going on and calling attention to what you see. By being keen observers for our planet, we are more connected to the world around us and in a better position to prevent harm and improve the health of the earth.

To lay out this territory, I will suggest several lenses for observing suffering in the environment. The more skilled you are in observing, the more you will be able to detect changes in the system. While this is not a comprehensive catalog of the realms of witnessing, it can be a place to begin.

Individual Suffering

One of the most natural ways to observe suffering is one on one, body to body. We feel empathic concern when we see a small child crying or a person who has lost a limb. When people we love are stricken with grief or illness, we want to be with them to offer support, to listen, to witness their suffering. That same response arises for some people when they see an animal or plant suffering. If you have a personal relationship with a companion animal, you become highly sensitized to the animal's behaviors and can quickly tell when that fellow creature is suffering. This skill is easier to develop with animals we are around all the time; it is much more challenging to do the same with wild animals. Wildlife biologists are trained professionally to recognize wild animal behavior and patterns of disease for different species. They spend hundreds of hours in the field observing wild animals, tracking their movement patterns, diet, and social relations to determine the state of their health. They are often the first people to spot outbreaks of disease such as West Nile virus, which has spread so quickly across the continent.

Without accurate knowledge of animal behaviors, we may misinterpret something we believe is an indicator of suffering. Or we may miss entirely some signals that can't be picked up by our sense organs. It is important to recognize that our witnessing capacities are limited by our own perceptual capacities. For example, we don't hear as well as most dogs and we can't see ultraviolet light like bumblebees. We see well in the daylight, like crows, but we don't see well at night like owls do. Further, no two human witnesses will have the same perceptual capacities. What we are able to perceive is strongly influenced by the conditioning of our minds. An experienced birdwatcher can distinguish many more birdcalls than the average person, for example. All observations are conditioned by the mental development of the brain and neural system of an individual, and every individual has been shaped by a unique set of influences, including gender, race, and culture. What appears to be animal suffering to one person may not be recognized by another. There is no such thing as "objective" observation. It is important to humbly acknowledge this fact to keep one's observations in perspective.

Nonetheless, with the help of microscopes, telescopes, and binoculars we can observe in detail many aspects of animal and plant life. What, then, would be some indication an individual is suffering? Signs of physical injury or poor health might be first to catch your attention. The deadly nature of DDT was discovered when scientists noticed that pelican eggs were cracking before the chicks could mature. The commonly used pesticide had been released offshore from an industrial plant and had built up in the local fish population. The pelicans ate the fish that ate the DDT, and the cumulative DDT blocked the calcium from forming eggshells thick enough to hold together. Pelicans kept laying eggs, but the population was plunging toward extinction.

Sometimes it is the sudden scarcity or even *absence* of organisms that causes alarm: where did they go? Songbird populations are especially good indicators of widespread environmental impact. People who count birds every year follow the trends of individual species to see which are in decline or have disappeared altogether. Observing absence may be a sad clue that another species has gone extinct or perhaps has changed its migration route or feeding area. Absence in one area needs to be correlated with information elsewhere to build a more complete picture of what is going on. Field naturalists and volunteers with the Audubon Society now have extensive databases of bird counts from around North America that allow for year-to-year tracking of population fluctuations.

Ecosystem Suffering

While some people are more attuned to witnessing the suffering of individuals, others have a gift for sensing an ecosystem as a whole or being alert to the processes that determine the health of the system. Very often extensive data may be required to verify a significant change or impact on a system. But local residents may notice the first signs of trouble—a strange color in the creek or an outbreak of disease. The witness who senses that something is "not right" can alert a professional response team to gather the necessary information. They can then call on environmental groups to engage their resources in the troubled situation.

Ecosystem health depends on functional flows of energy, water, and nutrients. The most direct way to witness energy flow is through watching the weather. Patterns in the weather from year to year determine energy and water flow in ecosystems. How much heat for how long? How much rain for how many days in a row? What are the cumulative impacts of a stalled weather system or an unusually hot summer? How is the climate changing in response to global warming?

Powerful weather events almost always generate environmental suffering for some organisms and ecosystems. People in northern Vermont will never forget the sound of snapping trees during the ice storm of 1998. It sounded like gunfire going off—*bam, bam, bam!* The air crackled with the sound of trees going down under the weight of the ice. Freezing rain had been falling for over three days across several thousand square miles of eastern Canada, northern New York, and New England. Most of the news coverage covered the extensive power outages caused by the loss of thirty-five thousand utility poles and a thousand steel pylons, leaving millions of people struggling to stay warm. The tree loss was unprecedented; Quebec's maple syrup industry was devastated, and many forests looked clobbered, with broken limbs and trunks in chaos everywhere. It took weeks of witnessing to collect the full picture of what had happened to the northern woodlands.

Nutrient flows (carbon, nitrogen, oxygen, sulfur) are more easily observed in the relations *between* organisms in an ecosystem. If rains are steady, producing plenty of milkweed nutrients for munching caterpillars, it will be a good year for monarch butterflies. Steady rains, though, will also foster molds in agricultural fields, making it a potentially bad year for strawberries. The green witness looks for possible strains on relationships within systems as indicators of environmental impact. Not all ecological relations are immediately apparent, but many can be seen by repeated observation: noting who is eating whom, who is hanging out with whom, who is serving as a home for others, and so on.

Many people develop an ecosystem view by simply living in one place for a while and watching what goes on. Countless alarm cries have been registered because of local knowledge of place, reinforced by "friends of" places and place-based school programs. Old-timers are particularly good resources of place-understanding because they have been witnesses over decades or generations. They carry the long view, a sense of the local ecosystem across time and its capacity to respond to disturbance.

Personal Views of Suffering

Our capacities to witness suffering are shaped by our "personal view"—the combination of ethical, religious, aesthetic, and other values-based responses we have developed to the natural world. This view may be informed by ecological knowledge or by religious training, family values, or a keen sense of beauty. The personal view touches something very deep and real. It is hard to encapsulate in words, though many philosophers and religious writers have tried. Artists and poets may do better at pointing to the mystery of the world that is so much larger than our own small views of it. I encourage those on the green practice path to study the origins of their own personal views in order to be more honest observers. It is impossible to keep your personal views from influencing your perception of environmental suffering. But that does not mean that personal views are necessarily an impediment. They may, in fact, strengthen your own sense of why it is important to draw attention to ecosystem degradation or species extinction.

It is especially useful to recognize your own cultural conditioning toward other-than-human beings and their suffering. Many people raised in the West have been taught to see forests and rivers primarily as resources for human beings. Human-centered bias can be one of the greatest deterrents to being fully present with other living beings. If you see the environment as primarily for human use—whether for food, shelter, recreation, or spiritual development—you may not see how other species suffer under the thumb of human dominance. If you see the environment as only plants and animals, you will overlook the struggle of indigenous peoples. If you see the environment as only wild places, then you miss the cultivated places, the agricultural ecosystems, the recreational sites that also need protecting. Observing one's personal views often means actively confronting counterproductive bias that works against clear seeing.

Our personal response to suffering has also been shaped by the strong emotions of our life experiences, particularly as young people. People who grow up in abusive households are especially sensitized. They may have witnessed abuse of household pets, behavior that is now known to be associated with spousal abuse. Under constant threat from emotional and physical bullying, they may find solace in empathic relationship with non-human beings. Those who take on the protector role in relation to family bullies often carry that same position into their environmental work. Children who have been exposed to a lot of suffering when young—whether from illness, death, or harassment—are often the most sensitive to animal and ecosystem suffering. I believe that personal reflection on your own history with suffering is an important piece of the green practice path. It represents your best effort to be a clear witness, aware of the influence of the ideas and experiences that have shaped you.

These three lenses—observing individual, ecosystem, and personal views of suffering—offer practical ways to engage environmental suffering. The witness on the green practice path will have no shortage of things to observe; this is quite easily a lifetime practice. It is one thing, however, for suffering to catch your attention. It is quite another to actually sit with it and try to grasp its full measure in your heart.

BEING WITH THE SUFFERING

Sometimes there is nothing to be done about the suffering we witness. We feel helpless, sad, overwhelmed, anxious. It is difficult to accept these feelings and know the suffering will likely continue. When we look around and see how widespread the suffering is for animals, trees, oceans, and forests, we can easily become discouraged. When this happens we need spiritual support for sustaining our gaze in the face of such helplessness. The eco-theologian Jay McDaniel speaks of "green grace" and "red grace" as ways to experience a sense of healing in relation to suffering. His sense of Christian sacrament is that which makes us whole in the midst of our brokenness. Green grace arises from spiritual contact with special places and a sense of awe for the earth as a miraculous whole. Red grace is core to the Christian experience of communion, the idea that right within the suffering of Jesus is the healing love of his wisdom. Red symbolizes the blood that has been spilled on the cross and reminds us that we, too, by our actions in the world, also cause suffering. By acknowledging our own part in the suffering, we accept our failings and, at the same time, resolve to develop our spiritual capacities to offer peace and kindness to the earth.

Very often our minds make it more difficult to be with the suffering directly. We get caught up in our anxiety or our desire for resolution, wishing things were different. Too much mental activity can prevent us from just being with the fact of the suffering. One of the most helpful spiritual practices for this state of mental unrest is walking meditation. At a retreat in northern California we incorporated walking meditation as a way to be with the suffering of the local forests. Here in the land of big trees, it was very disturbing to listen to the constant rumble of logging trucks above the retreat center. Load after load of fallen giants passed by day and night, causing me great mental torture. I kept thinking of the scalped redwood groves, the hundreds of years of evolutionary heritage hurtling toward whirring sawmill blades. Every tree tore at my heart; it seemed as if they were taking my family away. And there was nothing to be done, at least right then. So we walked slowly, one step at a time, breathing, calming the mind. At first it seemed to make no difference; my mind was still on fire. But as the day wore on, with one long session after another of walking meditation, I found a way to be with the trucks and also be calm, breathing with the suffering in my heart.

In some situations walking meditation may not be enough. Even with the support of others, the quiet breathing may seem too passive, too self-conscious. You may want to be more active to express the pain you feel in being with the suffering of the earth. This is the place for prayer, for song, for wailing—for speaking out loud the words that need to be said: *May this destruction cease! May we find a better way! May the song of the earth prevail!* The voice cries out, sending your true wishes into the universe, giving you courage to stay with the suffering. The prayer takes the form of melody, the melody picks up rhythm, and soon you have a song to keep you company.

> My words are tied in one
> With the great mountains,
> With the great rocks
> With the great trees,
> In one with my body
> And my heart.
>
> Do you all help me
> with supernatural power,
> And you Day
> And you, Night!
> All of you see me
> One with this world!
> —Yokuts Indian prayer[1]

The songs are there for us to find, so are the prayers. They are made out of the suffering and can be called forth when we most need them. Being with the suffering is not something to fear; it is actually the way through to deeper understanding.

TRACING SUFFERING TO SOURCE

Observing suffering and being with the suffering are important places to begin. Inevitably we want to know *why* an individual or ecosystem is ailing, especially if the consequences may be significant. We hope that the unhealthy situation may be reversible. If we can make the correct diagnosis of the ailment, then we can find the appropriate course of healing. This is the basic process in any medical assessment of disease. In Buddhist philosophy this diagnostic method is expressed as the Four Noble Truths, one of the very first teachings of the Buddha after his profound awakening.

The first of the Four Noble Truths points to the indisputable existence of suffering, that all beings are subject to suffering through birth, illness, old age, and death. These challenges come with the territory of being alive. They apply to all organisms and all ecosystems. Nothing is really permanent; the fact of continuous change means there will be some suffering in the simple effort to stay alive. The witness looks directly at this suffering as a personal practice in being with the environmental crisis. Thich Nhat Hanh's phrasing of this precept is very strong:

> Do not avoid contact with suffering or close your eyes before suffering. Do not lose awareness of the existence of suffering in the life of the world. Find ways to be with those who are suffering by all means, including personal contact and visits, images, sound. By such means, awaken yourself and others to the reality of suffering in the world.[2]

The second Noble Truth urges the practitioner to look deeply into the cause of the suffering at hand. Certainly not every form of environmental suffering has human action as a root cause. Landslides, earthquakes, and outbreaks of disease are the result of many physical and biological pressures on existing earth systems. They are not necessarily "fixable" by human intervention. But this suggests a method for tracing cause—look to the agents involved in the situation. If people are part of the picture, we can ask: Who is taking action and why? What is their motivation? What profitable activities are they trying to keep going? How are they "attached" to the things they are doing that cause harm to the earth? When we ask difficult and sometimes uncomfortable questions, it encourages close scrutiny of the situation and reveals insight into what is driving the suffering. Good critical thinking depends on a well-developed analytical mind. Scientific training develops such analytic skills, and so do Buddhist practice and other disciplines of the mind. By naming the specific agents (people, corporations, governments) driving a specific environmental harm, we can begin to map out root causes and their relative impacts.

This is not easy work. It can sometimes take years to sort out the history of actions that caused groundwater pollution or climate change. Even if the players and their actions are identified, there is often no momentum or social process for calling them to task. Sometimes it takes a change in political leadership before certain problems and problem-causers can be addressed. Sometimes it takes years and years of educating the public before there is enough pressure to stop the harming action. We are still in the middle of those years and years with climate change. Identifying root causes is crucial work because it is a powerful form of truth-telling. By naming the causes along with their specific agents, it becomes possible to assign responsibility and hold agents accountable for the consequences of their actions. This, in fact, was the foundational philosophy behind the 1980 U.S. Superfund Act—the principle that the "polluter pays." Climate negotiators from the South have adapted this principle to climate negotiations, insisting that northern countries pay for the damage their industrial economies have caused from carbon emissions.

The third Noble Truth states that there can be an end to the suffering. This is a message of hope and healing: it is possible to address the causes determined in the second diagnostic step. There is no guarantee of specific outcomes, but we do find strong affirmation of a complex universe that is in continuous flux. With multiple potential players and outcomes, something can happen that changes the current state of things for the better. From witness to analyst, the practice path now takes us to the role of active agent. Everyone has the capacity to offer some useful contribution that will turn the situation from harm to healing. The third Noble Truth affirms this capacity, encouraging us to be more confident that human beings can make a positive difference with the environment.

SKILLFUL ACTION

But how to act? What do the Four Noble Truths have to say about choice of action? The fourth Noble Truth describes a wheel of eight spokes, each of which helps to turn the dharma wheel of liberation. Right livelihood, right speech, right effort—these and the other spokes are specific places to practice healing. Right or skillful action is what leads to happiness, or we could say healthiness, as in the healthy functioning of an ecosystem. Unskillful actions tend to lead to unhappiness or unhealthiness. Skillful and unskillful action generates internal results, or how you feel about your choice of action, as well as external results, or the way it affects others. Sri Lankan teacher Bhante Gunaratana explains that skillful actions "are those that create the causes for happiness" and "bring happiness to the doer and receiver."[3]

Skillful action requires clear intention and some understanding of cause and effect. I suggest three additional criteria for choosing action steps. First, the action would be *appropriate*—that is, fitting in scale to the situation, within cultural norms of acceptance, and directly related to the suffering at hand. Second, the action would be *effective*—that is, it would make some difference in reducing the current suffering, and it would lead to further effective measures. Third, the action would be *doable* by a specific agent. It is useless to think of good solutions if there is no one in a position to actually carry them out. Actions are taken by people, and people have to be not only willing to take them but in a position where they are permitted or even supported to take them.

"What can you actually do?" This is an important question, useful in almost every situation, environmental or not. It may be true that every little action counts, but we need to look at *which* actions are most effective in the big picture of things. Often when I speak with students or in public lectures, people ask me: *How should I begin? What is the right thing for me to do?* I know it can seem overwhelming; there are endless possibilities for taking action. It is easy to become paralyzed just trying to consider where to step into the fray. Certainly some issues such as climate change seem to override smaller concerns such as styrofoam cups. But ultimately the suffering must call to you in some way. It must touch you, move you to want to be with the suffering, to analyze its causes, to find a course of action. That is a tall order of business. It desperately needs your heartfelt motivation. The call itself contains its own response.

I encourage people to begin by listening to the heart. What threat to life moves you most? What situation has come to your attention through a friend, a news article, a minister, a bike ride? What causes you to feel some moral twinge, some sense that you ought to be doing something? The situations are continuously presenting themselves; if one of them speaks especially loudly, that is the one to respond to. I have great faith in this approach to environmental work; I have seen it motivate people to do amazing things—from sitting atop tall redwoods for months at a time to planting trees in the middle of a desert. The process is iterative; it instructs as it unfolds. One response leads to another call, and that call leads to further response. Spiritual leaders speak of "following one's calling" as a way to be of service in the world. Skillful action based in call and response can be exactly that: one's calling to act on behalf of others so that the earth community may thrive.

Witnessing the suffering of the world impels us to step out of our individual lives and engage the bigger issues around us. When you start this work it is important to enter where you can be most effective in drawing on your own experience. If you sink in over your head you will not be very helpful. But if you can wisely listen to the voice in your heart, you will find your piece of the work. The invitations are all around us—which one calls to you? With a strong intention to reduce harm and be a witness to suffering, your steps on the green practice path can indeed make a difference. This ailing world is much in need of people who can see and respond to environmental suffering. Your sincere efforts are greatly needed—what can you offer to this world?

3

Embracing the Deep View

WE BEGAN THIS BOOK looking at how to reduce harm and how to be with harm as a witness and compassionate advocate for the earth. In this chapter we turn to wisdom insight—using the mind to understand the interdependent nature of reality, with systems thinking as a tool for analysis. The Buddha spoke of the two pillars of practice as compassion and wisdom. As we witness the suffering in the world around us, we see that cultivating a compassionate heart is crucial to the green path. But the heart alone can too easily be carried away with the depths of the suffering. The practiced systems thinker is able to balance a heart response with a wider view of the whole earth system, a view that acknowledges many contributing causes and conditions. Identifying agents and histories can illuminate the complex causes behind an environmental problem. Seeing things as interdependent and mutually co-arising can inform our compassionate urge to relieve suffering.

In traditional Chinese painting, landscape scrolls convey detailed images from multiple perspectives, offering the viewer many ways to enter the landscape. We are invited, for instance, to engage the intimacy of the near view in river-bank scenes or perhaps a small tea shelter. We are led to experience the high view from mountaintops and waterfalls. But the paintings also include a third perspective, what is called the "deep view." Here we look deep into the painting to see the inner folds of the mountains, the ridges behind ridges understood not literally but rather in the mind's eye. Embracing the deep view means looking beyond what you see at first glance, looking more deeply for the hidden structures and causes behind what we observe.

UNDERSTANDING ECOLOGICAL SYSTEMS

In every environmental educator's toolbox is a compass, a hand lens, binoculars, field guides, and also a ball of yarn. Yarn for what, you wonder? Not for measuring or marking off plots, not for identifying plants—no, this yarn is for the food-web game. Students stand in a circle, and the instructor begins by throwing the ball of yarn to one person while holding onto the leading edge. That person throws the ball to another person and so on, creating a criss-cross network of yarn strands linking the whole group together. The lesson is about how everything in the universe is tied together. Students sometimes hold signs to identify their role in the food web: grass, rabbit, snake, hawk. To show how the system works, the instructor tugs on one link (as if hoarding resources) and it pulls other links taut. Someone else drops the link she is holding (as if she is leaving the food web), and the line grows slack. To simulate pollution or disaster, the instructor has many students drop their links. Death takes its toll, and system relations grow thin.

The parallels with ecosystems are convincing; that is why this exercise is used over and over again for every outdoor science camp. After many teaching seasons with my own ball of yarn, I encountered a seventh-century Chinese Buddhist teaching from the Hua Yen school that used a house of mirrors as a metaphor. Something clicked in my mind. Was this not a much earlier version of the food-web game? In the scripture, Master Fa Tsang is trying to explain the nature of reality to the empress of China. Though the famed teacher had given a number of lectures on Buddhist philosophy, true realization had not yet penetrated the mind of the empress. So the teacher set up a demonstration in a palatial hall, placing mirrors on all four walls as well as the ceiling and floor. In the center of the hall he placed a small Buddha with a candle. The effect was to multiply the image of the Buddha ad infinitum wherever the empress looked. *Aha! A moment of insight!* The empress saw that the Buddha's mind is everywhere and infinite in its appearances throughout space and time.

Effective as this was, it was not a very portable lesson since it depended on having a hall of mirrors at hand. Thus, teachers developed another metaphor drawn from early Vedic literature to make the same point. "Indra's Net" was described as an enormous net stretching across the universe in all directions. To conceive of this in your own mind, visualize a huge fishnet of linked lines extending ad infinitum across horizontal space. Add a second net stretching across space vertically. And then imagine an endless number of nets crisscrossing every plane of space. At each node in every net, and at every point that the nets intersect, picture a multifaceted jewel reflecting every other jewel in the net. There is nothing outside the net and nothing that does not reverberate its presence throughout the net. Indra's Net is a truly marvelous conception—a universe of glittering jewels all linked together in one interwoven cosmos. The metaphor illuminates in a dramatic way the interdependent nature of reality, infinitely linked and infinitely co-reflecting.

Not surprisingly, this Buddhist concept was picked up by modern environmentalists, who saw it as a perfect representation of John Muir's famous words: "When we try to pick out anything by itself, we find it hitched to everything else in the universe." Indra's Net provided an understandable image for the ecological worldview in

a way that conveyed the awe and appreciation that environmentalists hoped to inspire in society. This metaphor has had particular
cachet among those who see a compatibility between ecological thinking and Buddhist thinking. Every link in the net represents a relationship in the myriad food webs of myriad ecosystems; every jewel
represents an organism, river, or mountain in the planetary web of life.
Tarnish a jewel with soot or sludge, and it shines much less brightly;
break a link with urban sprawl or clear-cutting, and ecological relations suffer.

I was completely enamored of this metaphor for a number of years
and happily shared it with whomever would listen. If I could have
built a demonstration model, I would have tried. But now I see it
would have fallen short of truly representing the dynamic nature of
reality. The net of jewels is a map or model but only of a single moment in time. To begin to conceive of the true nature of the universe, you would have to imagine all the nets in motion in a variety
of patterns and all the jewels changing constantly in size, shape,
behavior, and location. This brings us closer to reality, yet still it
falls impossibly short. In any given moment, the whole universe is
changing, morphing, growing, moving, learning, adapting beyond
any human comprehension. No single model can even come close
to capturing all that is going on.

If I were still teaching sixth-grade science camp, I would give up
my ball of yarn and offer the students a more dynamic experience of
systems in motion. In this exercise, we begin by forming a circle in a
wide open space.[1] Each person silently chooses two other people in
the group to follow as they move. The directions are simple: keep
yourself equidistant from the two people you are following. You can
be right in between them or equally far from both of them. When
the instructor says "go," everyone begins to move and the "system"
takes on a life of its own. The movement is impossible to predict
since it is the sum of all the simultaneous decisions of the participants.

It can be pretty funny to watch the group as people struggle to keep up with their reference points. Like the yarn game, this exercise can include variations, such as holding some players up in prison or refugee camps, thereby reducing the vitality of the moving system. Almost as interesting as the game is the debriefing afterward, when you ask people to explain what happened. They find it dumbfounding that such a complex pattern can arise from one simple rule.

This game gives people a taste of being part of a dynamic system. Even though the system's movement is governed by just one rule, it opens a window on the interdependent, spontaneous, dynamic, and infinitely complex nature of reality. Their imaginations can take the next step—what if there were two or three rules governing our behavior as members of the system? Of course, the instructor helps them remember that there are *many* physical, biological, cultural, economic, and political rules that people are following *all* the time in all of their interactions. Exercises such as this can help people develop a receptivity to systems thinking and a more flexible view of the universe.

THINKING ABOUT SYSTEMS

Why think about systems? How can this help us understand the nature of environmental problems or the way human beings are deeply tied to ecological systems in virtually everything they do? Actually, we are "thinking" about systems all the time; we just may not notice. Our minds and bodies have evolved in the context of ecosystems, climate systems, food webs, social systems—all of these are shaping and honing the human organism across time to be a successful animal. Our senses are constantly providing information on the state of the surrounding system—the color of the sky, the pace of traffic, the tone of family voices. We are responding to systems all the time and adjusting our behaviors accordingly. We all want to survive, and for the most part, that depends on fitting in with the systems we must relate to. Formal systems thinking builds on this animal body level of knowing that is already embedded in our limbic brain from many years of evolution. With our highly developed neocortex, we can study and observe systems and develop useful mental skills in recognizing systems behavior.

Austrian biologist Ludwig von Bertalanffy (1901–1972) was one of the first people to articulate general systems theory in the West. He called it "a way of seeing." Working in the 1930s, he found that reductionist approaches to biology fell short in describing organism behavior. He saw each plant and animal as a whole, not so much a thing as a pattern of flows in space and time. Each being was not only whole in itself but was also part of a whole system, being shaped by it and also shaping it in turn. He also saw human beings as wholes, rejecting mechanistic views of human behavior and laying the groundwork for Gestalt and other systems-oriented psychologies yet to come. He characterized nature as an open system, with flows of matter, energy, and information passing through constantly. His term for this flow was *Fliessgleichgewicht,* which means "flux-balance." [2]

But what is it that is in flux-balance? In the Chinese worldview, the entire cosmos consists of dynamic energy fields, constantly in flux and driven and permeated by *ch'i,* which is sometimes translated as "vital force or power." This flowing energy fills the universe and is present in all material forms. From moment to moment, it is constantly transforming, shape-shifting, becoming, unfolding. The Chinese term to match Bertalanffy's flux-balance is *sheng-sheng-pu-yi*—"incessant activity of life creativity." [3] We can compare Chinese and Western views of environment and see that our understanding of systems will be very different depending on our assumptions and worldviews. Western views tend to be more mechanical and atomistic: we speak of "environment" as our surroundings, the background to our everyday activities, something that is relatively inert, except for occasional big surprises such as earthquakes and hurricanes. In contrast, the Chinese view encompasses much more: it includes the deep structure and process of life itself—sometimes visible, often hidden. In the Chinese classic text, the Tao Te Ching, the Tao, which is "nowhere not present," is the true environment for all human and ecological activity.

This dynamic view offers a broad foundation for viewing harm and sources of harm. The systems view helps us to think about not just ecosystems but also social systems, economic systems, and political systems. It calls for a much more comprehensive response to environmental concerns than do traditional views. A surface-level cleanup of a polluted river or an oil spill may solve the immediately visible problem, but what about all the contributing systems that generated the problem in the first place? If we take a deep view based in the ever-flowing ch'i, we may be more likely to find root causes. We are also far more likely to see ourselves as real players in the whole story, players whose habitual actions generate significant consequences.

OBSERVING SYSTEMS BEHAVIOR

There is no one approach to observing systems; biologists and sociologists each have their own tools, ministers and athletic coaches have come up with others. To develop a systems mind you begin by looking at the fundamental qualities or behaviors of systems. This work is gratifying because learning in one arena easily translates to other settings. If you are a gardener, you can practice observing the systems of your garden—the plant-animal relations, the soil systems, the weather. If you are a parent, you can practice observing your family system—the sibling relations, the weekly rhythms, the changing needs of each person over time. As you use the lens of systems thinking, you will build capacity to understand nature and environmental concerns as systems—intertwining, overlapping, cross-influencing, and more complex than we can yet explain. This way of seeing offers a very powerful counterweight to the fragmenting, separating views so entrenched in Western approaches.

Let's look at some basic aspects of systems. First, the whole (system) is greater than the sum of the parts. In other words, if you took the system apart and only looked at its parts, you would no longer have systemic-level behavior. The system as a whole has its own unique qualities that are not necessarily represented in the parts. A living, breathing human being, for example, is composed of tissues and organs. The heart pumps blood, the lungs inhale and exhale, but neither of them alone is able to run, love, or cook. A coral reef is filled with many colorful coral communities in wild and dazzling shapes, but a single polyp alone does not produce the dance of tropical fish and crabs that fill a reef.

Second, every system is composed of subsystems and is itself part of a larger system. Planetary systems exist within galaxies, cells within tissues, nurse logs within forests. These can be mapped or modeled in various ways. We have the branching tree metaphor of evolution and taxonomy or the metaphor of rivers and watershed. Another model is that of nested boxes, like the set of ten Russian dolls someone gave me, one inside the other—all the way down to the teeny tiniest. We could think of the knotted fishnet, the Indra's Net model of systems relations, or some of the many electronic models for information storage and access. Some models imply a set of hierarchical relations; others are more free form.

To practice systems thinking, you start with almost anything and look at what systems it is part of and what systems it contains. When I look out my window toward Mount Mansfield, I see the peak as part of the Green Mountain ridge that runs north-south through Vermont. Or I could see it as part of the cell phone grid sending signals from its high point to link up with other signals. Or I see it as a major ski area within the Vermont winter recreation system. If I drive up the winding toll road, I could see each altitudinal bioregion, climb-ing from the oak-beech-maple forest into the balsam firs and pines, and on up to the stunted, gnarled trees and moss gardens of the rocky peak. Pick a single moss garden, and get down on your hands and knees—worlds within worlds appear. Tiny pools connected by minia-ture waterfalls, insects hiding in the shadows, a small stone with its own world of lichens. The world becomes quite magical—how can there be so much going on? This experience is at the root of much re-ligious experience, the sense of awe and wonder invoked by the sheer complexity of it all. Words fail; a sense of the mystical takes over. This practice is what my husband calls "Big Fun," delighting in the deep view of the universe. Of course, the same practice yields heartrending insight when applied to systems of war, injustice, or poverty. I can also look out my window to Mount Mansfield and see the Green Moun-tain Air Guard flying over in tight formation as part of a defense sys-tem that is part of a national government that must procure oil, no matter what the environmental cost.

Two more aspects of systems behavior relate to how a system main-tains itself and how it responds to changing conditions. These behav-iors are fundamental to all organisms—finely tuned self-maintenance and adaptability as needed in order to survive. Without well-devel-oped behaviors that maintain stability, the system unravels. Our most fundamental physiology as human beings is regulated to sustain regular breathing, steady heart rates, and balanced chemical flows. Forests, too, are stabilized by internal processes of soil chemistry and decomposi-tion. Unfortunately, there is no such a thing as "the balance of nature," a fuzzy phrase that mostly reflects wishful thinking. But there are highly evolved feedback mechanisms within any given system that provide constant information about how the system is doing. You know this from your own experience. Feeling a little chilly on a cool autumn night? Put on a sweater. Getting too hot from the Indian curry? Have some cooling yogurt. Dampening (or negative) feedback generally communicates the message *Had enough? Then have a little less.* We, and all other living beings, are constantly and actively adjusting our behaviors and internal chemistry to maintain as close to optimal state as possible.

But our usual behaviors aren't always appropriate if conditions change. (And conditions are always changing.) To see what works in a new circumstance, we try something and wait for feedback. If the message is *Good, that works, do more,* then we keep going with the new behavior, which seems to be more effective in the new circumstance. This is the basic mechanism in learning; teachers and parents who know how to give amplifying (or positive) feedback are very effective in reinforcing the behaviors and skills they see as valuable. Ecosystems too are constantly adapting to changing conditions and responding to amplifying feedback in various forms. A meandering river channel will push farther into the bank along the inside of a curve at peak flow. If it is a season of heavy rain, the forceful currents will change the shape of the channel to meet the raging river. Positive feedback that enhances the flows in the system can be good, as in a boom year for pollinators. But amplifying feedback in runaway mode means a system is out of control and no longer able to meet the changing conditions—waterlogged soil turns to landslide, brush fire becomes holocaust. We can also see runaway feedback in addictions, when more alcohol, more sugar, or more war is no longer effective and the system destabilizes into chaos.

One way to understand feedback relations in a system is through disturbance. Northern forests are regularly disturbed by avalanches and ice storms that cause physical havoc, and insect invasions that cause biological distress. If a system can recover quickly from the disturbance, we say it is "resilient." We see how quickly young trees grow back in the gaps left by the storm. We see how insect predators multiply to feed on the invaders. You can observe this in your own family system. What happens when a small crisis passes through? Which members of the family weather it well and who takes a long time to recover? For those who are more sensitive, is there a way to build their resilience (confidence, immune system, inner strength)?

Yet another lens for understanding systems is through examining the role of borders and centers. What gets in, what goes out? And through what gates, by what messages? Who lives at the center, who prefers the edges? If the gates or borders change, through clear-cutting, for example, how does it change the forest as a compatible home for its usual inhabitants? All defense systems, biological and otherwise, are about defending borders and centers. You can observe your own defense systems—your tone of voice when irritated, or the way you respond to catching cold. You can also think about how you defend yourself from painful information about the environment and how you manage media flows coming in through your mental gates. Observing systems at whatever level available to you is very instructive. What you learn about one system will not necessarily apply directly to another system, but the learning process itself builds capacity for understanding other systems.

Once we understand the systems around us, we can better understand how to influence those systems and create positive change. Many people in the world have taken the initiative to help restore forest ecosystems and mitigate global warming through planting trees. Last year alone, members of the Arbor Day Foundation planted over eight million trees, engaging citizens in many towns and regions in the re-greening of the landscape. Where forests have been decimated by harvest operations, tree-planting establishes vegetative cover that in turn protects soil from washing away. Where skyscrapers and asphalt have turned cities into urban heat islands, tree-planting adds cool shade, which reduces the heat buildup in summer. By being active agents in Indra's Net, we can invest in ecosystem restoration, reversing the runaway degrading feedback and helping the system recover positive growth and stability. At the same time, our actions generate a personal sense of well-being, reinforced by positive feedback.

SYSTEMS VIEW OF SELF

What if we apply all that I've been saying to our views of the self? How are we to understand the self from a systems point of view? Very quickly we see that "self" is not what we have been told. We don't really operate independently with free will governing our actions, not if we are a part of multiple systems. Each of us reflects the day's weather and the mood in our household. We act from the legacy of our parents' values and the deeply familiar psychological habits of our families of origin. We speak from our knowledge of woods and streams or oceans and beaches. We offer an opinion as a member of a company or agency. Looking closely at our situation, it becomes obvious: we don't exist apart from these systems. Understanding this powerful and basic truth is critical to the green practice path.

As a practicing Buddhist, I am particularly interested in this question of self. And as an environmentalist, I want to know what motivates people to take action. This takes us back to "call and response." We hear the calls of environmental celebration or distress because we are always receiving information through the systems we are part of. If the call is reinforced (with amplifying feedback) then it carries more weight, and we are willing to invest our time in responding. If we perceive ourselves as part of a larger system acting through us, then we put less weight on our own needs and perspectives, taking more of a whole earth perspective.

One of the first systems thinkers to catch the attention of environmentalists was biologist Gregory Bateson. In his book, *Steps to an Ecology of Mind,* he used the activity of woodcutting to illustrate this systems view of self.[4] As the woodcutter for our household in California, chopping wood was one of my favorite chores. I loved the swing of the ax in my hand, the smell of the freshly split wood, the beautiful chips piling up around the stump. Stacking wood is an aesthetic delight for me, requiring care at every placement to keep the weight and balance just right in the stack. Bateson described the actions of chopping wood as being located not just in the person but in the "total self-corrective unit" that is continually receiving feedback from the ax, the chopping block, the wood, the eyes and brain, the muscles at work in the chopping. That's what I love about chopping wood. By training my mind on the whole information loop— wood to eye to arm to ax—I actually perceive the flow of feedback, I see myself as part of a circuit of energy. I see the wood correcting me, I see the ax teaching me how to use its weight, I see my breath chopping the wood through the ax.

Bateson's work went unnoticed by most psychologists in the 1970s, but his understanding of systems feedback informed later developments in the field. In their book titled *A General Theory of Love,* Thomas Lewis, Fari Amini, and Richard Lannon described what they called "limbic regulation." The limbic brain, situated above the brain stem and beneath the neocortex, is the center of emotional response to the external world. Limbic signals influence physiological functions that keep us ready to deal with what comes our way. Limbic regulation is a mutual simultaneous exchange of body signals that unfolds between people who are deeply involved with each other, especially parents and children. The authors suggest that you may be most stable as a social human if you have well-developed synchronization with nearby loved ones. Their work implies that people can't be completely stable outside a social system because they are too deprived of feedback. Self-sufficiency is a myth. They recommend finding people "who regulate you well" and then staying near them.

This neurological research provided insights about more than emotion and love. The studies showed that learning itself depends on limbic regulation. Monkeys raised in isolation develop different brain chemistry from monkeys raised in a social environment and are prone to despair and anxiety. Children raised with love (which translates as high limbic engagement) develop more stable memory capacity than those who are abused. Memory is the activity of making neural links that together add up to recognition. Held securely in the stable limbic signaling of love, children are more able to build up linking bits of information in the brain and retain important patterns of information. The letters of the alphabet "stick." A child puts together color, shape, and smell to mentally see the object described by the word "flower." The limbic feedback in the family system provides stability that then supports the feedback of learning. If his or her primary relations are emotionally troubled, a young child's neural chemistry is less stable, which then affects the capacity to learn.

We could take this work a step further from a systems perspective, and imagine that a child also learns through some sort of limbic regulation with nature. If we take the Chinese worldview of flowing ch'i, the systems circuitry Bateson described is also happening between people, plants, and animals. Our "self " is then a flowing stream of information and communication with all those we live with. Deep ecologist Bill Devall calls this the "ecological self" or the "true self." Mitch Tomashow writes of our "ecological identity," the way we recognize this flowing stream in our individual experience. Zen teacher Thich Nhat Hanh speaks of "interbeing," the self that co-exists and co-arises with all other life.[5]

In order to counter the terrible mountain of despair and helplessness we may feel in facing environmental abuse, it is important to remember that each of us is a participating agent in these energetic loops; we can help shape the loops through action and feedback. Agency is everything in a world with so many challenges. Even as the feedback is shaping us, we are shaping the feedback and the shape of the systems we are part of. We are learning and adapting, and we are influencing others to follow our model through limbic resonance. When we model environmental responsibility, we are not just being virtuous; we are creating a limbic opportunity to influence others. Understanding the world in this way, we can use positive feedback with intention to care more effectively for the systems we are part of.

PERCEIVING DEEP TIME

So far I have said very little about time or perceiving systems as manifestations of events in time. Our experience of time is so tied to our
own human life spans that it can be difficult to comprehend other
scales of time. In the twenty-first century, time only seems to be accelerating. Slow or long views of unfolding situations can seem out of
grasp in our harried world. To see systems as they change across time
requires a conscious effort to step back from the present-moment
viewpoint.

One of my environmental heroes, Rachel Carson, had a master-
ful sense of time. Though most people know her primarily for her
monumental 1962 work, *Silent Spring,* her understanding of time is represented soulfully in her earlier sea books. She was at heart a marine
biologist, happy to spend hours and hours walking along Atlantic
coast beaches or poking around in Maine tide pools. Though she did
not use these terms, she was clearly a systems thinker with a deep view.
Her sea writing is infused with a felt sense of time operating at all
scales, from the ephemeral to the geologic. She had the remarkable
ability to suspend identification with her own life span and enter fully
into the experience of time as manifested in tide-pool anemones or
the movement of glaciers. Her close observation of the monthly and
yearly tide rhythms kept her in contact with the cosmic movements
of the sun, moon, and earth. She felt her studies of the constantly
changing shoreline kept her own life in proper perspective.

> For the differences I sense in this particular instant of time
> that is mine are but the differences of a moment, determined
> by our place in the stream of time and in the long rhythms of
> the sea. Once this rocky coast beneath me was a plain of sand;
> then the sea rose and found a new shore line. And again in
> some shadowy future the surf will have ground these rocks to
> sand and will have returned the coast to its earlier state."[6]

A deep time view may come more naturally to those who watch butterflies or explore the shapes of rivers and mountains over time. Geologists and evolutionary biologists have much to offer us in this regard. They look for clues that tell something about the nature of systems operating in other eras and climates. They describe patterns in rock formation or erosion that may account for evidence of earlier such events. They are able to see present time intermingled with past time and imagine also future time—how an eroding mountain will eventually crumble to the sea over thousands of years. Perceiving time this way is a cultivated skill. It takes patience and repeated practice in seeing across time, helped along by those more experienced and gifted in this way of seeing.

The Dominican cofounder of Genesis Farm, Sister Miriam MacGillis, has developed a deep time exercise to give people a sense of cosmic and evolutionary time. It is similar to the experience of walking a labyrinth pattern, in and back, finding your way through the maze one step at a time. For this "cosmic walk" the path is set up in a spiral, with points along the way to mark key events in the creation of the universe. Each point is marked by a burning candle and a small card. As people walk the spiral, they pause at each candle to read the next event in the story, beginning with the first flaring forth of the Big Bang. The walk is held in silence to allow each person to find his or her own experience of what Father Thomas Berry calls "the universe story." Yet everyone is walking together, all part of the story being told again in a new way. This ritual walk calls up the experience of systems over time, the larger temporal contexts we are part of. As I walked this spiral with my students, each candle, each important moment of the universe story opened a glimpse of deep time. I could feel in my mind and body a sense of immensity, that these gifts of time—our sun, the planets and stars, our home earth— were the results of systems within systems operating across many timescales.

In the Flower Ornament Sutra, the Buddha speaks of "ten penetrations" as yet another deep view of time and existence. The culminating tenth aspect is: "All times penetrate one time. One time penetrates all times—past, present, and future. In one second, you can find the past, present, and future."[7] What are we to make of this seemingly mystical teaching? Thirteenth-century Zen master Eihei Dogen took this up in his essay on Time-Being. "Each moment is all being, is the entire world. Reflect now whether any being or any world is left out of the present moment."[8] From a systems perspective, this is deeply logical. The traces of systems activity reflect what has come before (the cumulative feedback), and the current systems as we see them are in this very moment shaping what will arrive in the future.

This deep view of time reinforces a sense of self as process more than thing, a sense that we are always arising, right alongside all other beings spontaneously becoming themselves as well. Within this dynamic universe of existence, we are very much situated in systems of time and space. And it is within these specific systems we are able to act. As participating agents in political, economic, family, and environmental systems, we *can* make a difference. The evidence is all around us. How will we *choose* to act?

PART TWO

Following the Green Path

4

Entering the Stream

REDUCING HARM, being with the suffering, embracing the deep view—these three principles provide a practical and philosophical orientation to the green practice path. Keeping these in mind, we can see how they might guide our steps along the path. But what exactly is that path? How do we understand what it means for us personally to be on a green path? Is it primarily a matter of lifestyle, or does it involve our family care and livelihoods as well? How far should we take these green principles? Wrestling with these questions may not be easy, but it is very helpful in determining what we can actually accomplish on the green path in our own lives.

In this chapter I look at stages of development along the green practice path, sharing my observations from working with students, colleagues, and environmentally concerned citizens. Each person experiences green zeal in different ways and to different degrees across his or her life. The green practice path is necessarily very broad, for people are finding many ways to walk this path. One step leads to the next, and then somehow to the next, a journey specific to each person. Walking together on the path with others, the call grows louder and the commitment deepens.

In my introductory class in environmental studies, we invite a number of local environmentalists to panel sessions to tell their stories and share their current work in the field. The guests range from professionals with years of experience to student peers engaged in campus issues. For their homework the students interview some-one involved in environmental work, asking questions about their experience and motivation. I want young people to hear up close the adventure, the doubt, the twists and turns of how an individual path unfolds. The stories they hear become alluring hooks, encouraging the young explorers to keep going, to see what lies ahead. They come to see that environmental work is all about people, each person in his or her own way, trying to find a way to respond to their concerns.

In another course, we look at the lives of key thinkers in the environmental field—Henry David Thoreau, Aldo Leopold, Rachel Carson, Wendell Berry, Bill Devall, Karen Warren, among others. I talk about Thoreau's cabin, Leopold's "shack," Carson's cottage in Maine, and how these small, private spaces supported their reflection and writing. I share the tragedy of Leopold's death by heart attack in a grass fire, before he could publish his now-famous collection of essays, *Sand County Almanac* (1949), and the terrible irony of Rachel Carson's breast cancer, draining her vitality even as she was writing *Silent Spring*. We consider the geographies, the education, the class and social background of these thinkers and the people who influenced them. Together we see that their ideas are a direct expression of a lived commitment to the work. We could say that these forebears are some of our role models on the green practice path.

Telling these stories, it can seem as if the practice path is composed of a series of steps, each leading to the next opportunity. At one level this is true; we can show the contours of our path by mapping the most significant steps that have steered the course of our lives. Each of us has our high peaks of achievement and low valleys of sorrow. We have all taken forks in the road that led to unexpected places. But the "winding path" metaphor overlooks the dynamic nature of what is unfolding in every moment. In the immediate experience

of walking the path, you are struggling with internal conflicts, hesi-
tations, fears, distractions. You don't know what lies ahead; by turns
you feel brave, lonely, assured, and resistant. You can't be sure you are
progressing or developing in your practice. You make an effort any-
way, and only later do you see which among your efforts has turned
out to be significant.

Around my home are a number of small figures of the bodhisattva
Kuan Yin, also known as Kannon, the bodhisattva archetype of compassion and skillful means. In her hands she offers various means of
assistance—a wish-fulfilling jewel, a vessel of soothing water, a lotus
of merit. In a piece titled *Kitchen Kannon,* the Japanese silk-screen artist
Mayumi Oda portrays a bodhisattva holding a whisk, a frying pan, a
spatula, and a fork—all to accomplish her cooking practice on behalf
of all beings. Some of the more elaborate Kannon statues have up to
a thousand arms, all ready to help in any way possible. One Kannon,
the Eleven-Faced Avalokiteshvara, is striking with its stack of heads,
each with three faces. Those facing to the front are calm and serene,
radiating kindness. Those on the left are wrathful and protective,
while those on the right have fangs to protect the earnest seeker.
Some scholars have suggested that the eleven faces or heads repre-
sent the ten stages of bodhisattva development described in the
Flower Ornament Sutra.[1] In that text the devoted bodhisattva is
working tirelessly to save the many suffering beings, but each time
she looks back, she sees even more beings arriving to take the place
of those she has saved. This causes her head to split apart with grief.
Over and over, her head breaks open, each grief greater than the
last. After the tenth time, the benevolent Amitabha, the buddha of
infinite light and potential, gives her his own head, and she is able to
continue her tireless work.

This bodhisattva's story seems to describe the green practice
path. In the middle of trying to do something useful for the earth,
you feel alternately calm or wrathful or protective of what you've accomplished. You think you are following a practice path with clear

intention, but the challenges seem only to multiply beyond your capacity. Your head or heart may be splitting apart with grief, but then others come forward to help, and you return to the work. Over the long term the practice of environmental work develops character and wisdom, but in each situation that may not be so apparent. All you can work with is the present moment. And that is everything. Each choice, each reflection, each consideration of what is appropriate nourishes the inner personal transformation that comes from taking up a path of practice.

A PATH OF PRACTICE

When people start out on the green path, environmental issues can feel like a separate world, something very much apart from their own lives. That sense of separation makes it harder to find a way to become part of the work in an effective and meaningful way. In a world of myriad environmental challenges, it is not always clear where to make a contribution. How do you know where to put your effort? How can you tell if your work is making a difference? As you look for a way to address our planetary situation, it is important to keep asking such questions until the appropriate answers arrive.

You might wonder where exactly to apply the green principles we've discussed. Should you work with a nonprofit organization or a government agency? Should you get a new, more green job? Should you work locally, nationally, or internationally? Hardly ever does anyone survey all the possible options and then make a rational decision about "what is best." There is too much going on; there is too much to know. This may seem overwhelming as you step onto the green path, but actually it is a good thing. We have come a very long way since the word "ecology" made its debut in the 1960s. In the twenty-first century, understanding ecology is central to sustaining life on earth as we know it. There are many conversations, many opportunities, and many good causes at every possible scale of engagement. The key is finding the right "fit" with your knowledge, skills, interest, and values. It also helps if someone extends you a hand.

Being naïve can be an advantage to the seeker. You approach any new topic of earth-keeping with a fresh mind, a willing curiosity, and your own humble honesty about how little you know. This means you must turn to others to learn more, coming with open hands as a student. Everything you encounter has some value because you don't yet know what will be useful. Beginner's mind is a beautiful gift for those entering the stream or taking up a new phase of the work. By asking for help or information, you take small steps in building relationships with others doing this work. This is very important; it is too easy to become discouraged if you try to go it alone in facing environmental issues. Forging connections with others makes it seem possible to do the work; those with experience are a testimony of success to surviving the challenges.

For some, the call or invitation comes first from the natural world itself. In my own formative years in environmental work I lived on the edge of a wild area near the University of California in Santa Cruz. I would often go for walks among the coastal live oaks on the grassy terraces or down to the dark canyon of the redwood-lined creek. During the long and emotionally demanding process of completing my graduate studies, I took my unshaped questions to the land, letting my feet guide me as I walked. I learned to respond to the pulls in different directions, not knowing where I would end up, trusting the process for its own wisdom. Sometimes I would find myself climbing an oak on the mesa for the big view of ocean and sky. Sometimes I would crawl close to a small spring nestled in moss, feeding the creek drop by drop. I found answers through listening closely, waiting for insight that made sense in a way I could recognize.

Some find the call arising from conversations with friends or from watching a stirring film. A neighbor tells you about her community garden plot; a colleague explains his house insulation project. After the widespread showing of Al Gore's 2006 film, *An Inconvenient Truth,* many people suddenly felt called to take up the challenge of climate change. For some, the response is quiet and personal, an inner reflection or reckoning: *It's time, I must do something.* For others, the process of taking up the green path is social and full of excited possibility, like the coming together of thousands of students involved in the Focus the Nation actions on climate. The sheer social momentum of so much inspiring activity can galvanize a crowd to new levels of green commitment.

This seeking or calling process generates a need to know more, to see who's doing what, to get your bearings in an unfamiliar universe. These days it is not hard to develop a basic working knowledge of ecological principles and to learn about key areas of concern where people are engaged as citizens and professionals. Information is quite accessible on the internet or in introductory books or environmental magazines. Many environmental groups welcome volunteers interested in broadening their knowledge base by working with others who know more. It can be tempting to want to study until you feel you know enough to take action. But if you get bogged down with information overload, it might undermine the forward momentum you are trying to generate. To counter this hazard, you should keep an eye on what I call your "juice meter." Which topics and issues generate energy for you? When do you notice your enthusiasm barometer going up? These moments offer important feedback in the learning process; they tell you what to pursue and what to leave for others to pursue. You don't even need to know why something is exciting, you just need to follow that thread to the next step.

In any given problem-solving arena, the question will arise: What is effective action? This is another way of asking: What can I actually do? How can I be effective, given who and what I know now? How can my work have some impact? These are important questions that should always be kept nearby in evaluating your potential to contribute, which, of course, is constantly changing. The newcomer to any environmental topic has a thousand ideas of "what people should do" to "save the environment." The good news is that most of these ideas are already in progress somewhere. You don't need to reinvent the wheel, you just need to find people who are already acting on your good ideas and join them. Chances are that they will already have assessed the options for effective action and will have developed initiatives that fit the current situation. People with more knowledge and experience, whether they are with the Sierra Club or the Department of Environmental Conservation or the local recycling center, have already given these matters quite a bit of thought.

The most important aspect in the early stages of the green practice path is to find what is personally satisfying and meaningful. Without this, you won't continue the work. It is also crucial to make some friends in the process. Without friends, you will feel isolated and lonely and the work won't be as much fun. People don't usually think of environmental practice as "fun," but if you are spending time with good people and sharing a sense of purpose, you are having a good time helping to create a more sustainable world. Whether you take up this work in your family setting or as a volunteer, in school or downtown, it is all useful. It is all part of the process of shifting the social paradigm toward active care for the place where you live, the place you call home. Your early experiences with green practice often set the direction for where the path leads you next, which may be further into the fray.

DEEPENING THE PRACTICE

Being a beginner with any environmental topic, by definition, cannot last. The more you know about the environment, the less you can rest in blissful ignorance. It is too disturbing. The more you know about climate change, threatened species, energy needs, and human impact, the more concern you are likely to feel. The more time you spend in beautiful natural areas, the more you find out about the physical and political threats to their well-being. The more you understand about social inequity and environmental injustice, the harder it is to see your own actions in isolation. Environmental knowledge can be a double-edged sword: learning more about the world's suffering often generates alarm and emotional distress. At the same time that very knowledge can galvanize you to take action and put that knowledge to work to alleviate suffering.

As a beginner you may have ventured into environmental work in a single arena such as food or caring about a personally significant place. Your shift to green thinking may have come from a single bout of intense commitment or smaller explorations at a gradual pace. If you stay on the green practice path, your range of interests and concerns will expand. If your interest has been sparked through organic foods, you might want to learn more about eating local. If you are concerned about the health impacts of pesticides, you might want to learn more about hormone disrupters. At some point you realize you are asking the green question more and more often. What is the environmental impact of this product? Of this housing development? Of this zoning policy? You realize you are no longer living in a bubble as if your actions had no impact anywhere. You know they do. Your environmental innocence is gone.

This is how a person enters the next stage of the path of practice. You may not have planned on it. You may find yourself surprised by your own growing convictions. Or you may be wondering how to become a more effective advocate for the environment. As a professor I am invited to be part of such wonderings, as students come to me considering graduate school or midcareer professionals ask about switching fields. Each person arrives in my office carrying a bundle of questions and possible options. They want to think out loud with someone and find something that matches their yearning. I ask them what has brought them this far on the path, and then I try to gauge what level of commitment they imagine for themselves. I listen while they share what they have been thinking about, no matter how tentative their vision. They have come for encouragement, to hear someone say, "Keep going, yes, you can do more." It is clear they want a wider engagement with environmental concerns in their personal or professional lives, or maybe even both.

Taking up this phase of deeper commitment involves several significant inner processes that inform each other. When the green critique penetrates further into your life, you may need to rethink personal priorities. Every day and every hour we are making choices that reflect our current priorities. We choose to invest our time, energy, money, relationships in certain things over others. Rethinking priorities means examining our current patterns and seeing if they really reflect what matters most to us. If environmental concerns come to occupy more of your everyday thoughts and activities, then it makes sense to move them more into the forefront of your activities. For example, you might learn enough about eating local foods to decide to grow some food of your own. This then means investing in a garden plot and in tools, seeds, soil amendments, compost box, and so on. It also requires an investment of your own precious and limited time. As you share the fruits and vegetables of your labors with others, success generates its own momentum and your investment pays off.

Rethinking priorities leads naturally to the second process of personal assessment. From those early stages of beginner's mind, you now have accumulated new skills and knowledge and likely have developed ethical stances in the areas where you have some understanding. So you ask yourself: *What do I know? What can I actually do? What more do I need to be helpful on another level?* It can be very useful to talk this through with someone who can be a witness to your personal growth as a concerned earth citizen. As much as you see what you have gained thus far, it will be obvious that there is much more to learn. It is not possible to do it all, no matter how concerned you are. You are only one person with a finite number of hours to give to earth care. So you must make some strategic choices to guide your next steps. For some people, what is appropriate is more education and professional development to prepare for full-time work in an environmental field. This is a common motivation for seeking a graduate degree. Others may need a change of location, a geographical move to bring them closer to a hub of environmental activity, such as Washington, D.C., or one of the rising centers of sustainability, such as Portland, Oregon. Still others may want a major change in lifestyle or more spiritual training to support deeper environmental work.

Complementing both of these processes is self-reflection on the Big Picture: *What is really important now, both in my own life and in the world?* When I was preparing to take lay ordination vows in the Soto Zen tradition, I was asked to do just this. My Zen teacher had me sit in a room quietly all day by myself, thinking about what it meant to take these vows. I felt somehow there was much more going on than I completely understood. I read the Buddhist precepts and recited the three refuges, settling my mind on accepting this commitment as best I could. In late afternoon I took a long slow walk in the New Mexico landscape, preparing to cross through this gate. The next day, after a light snow had dusted the mountains, I repeated my vows in the presence of the local Zen community and received affirmation from my teacher. Afterward we held a wonderful party, and one of my teacher's senior students called in on the phone to offer congratulations. He explained that before this day I had been practicing primarily for myself, to improve my own physical and mental well-being. Now, with these vows, my practice would be primarily in the service of others. When you come to take environmental work seriously, you realize you are doing it on behalf of all beings, not just for your own well-being. Looking at the Big Picture means understanding the nature of the current threats, seeing who the political players are, finding the initiatives that make the most sense in the long run. It also means really trying to apply global principles of justice and sustainability. We cannot do effective environmental work without taking up the roles of race, class, gender, power, and privilege in perpetuating environmental damage and inequity.

In the last few years the global conversation has shifted to focus on the impacts of climate change. All other environmental work seems to be subsumed or compared to the call to "do something" about climate change. Many of us find ourselves falling short in knowledge or skill to respond to this call and perplexed at how to shift personal priorities. Reflecting on the Big Picture of climate change, peak oil, and the exploding demand for resources is very unsettling. It is a time of great foment, with many ideas surfacing, many big conversations at play that will affect all of us. We are all being invited into this second stage of the practice path, with no time to waste.

TAKING UP THE PATH

For some people, and certainly not for all, there will be a third stage of the green practice path. At this point the practice becomes a "lifeway." In Native American traditions, people speak of everyday practice and culture fused into a way of life, something practiced by the whole community.[2] The lifeway includes ethics, spirituality, social mores, and a deeply tested way of doing things that makes sense. A lifeway is not a religion, it is not something you can adopt or be baptized into. A lifeway is also not an identity, in the sense of ethnic or political identity. A lifeway is a way of being in the world that carries strong intention and shared wisdom. People who follow a shared lifeway help each other develop this wisdom and the strength to persevere under duress.

To introduce my class to this idea of lifeway, I invite my friend Amy Seidel to visit as a colleague and role model. Amy is the director of Teal Farm, a demonstration site in northern Vermont for living sustainably in the future. Each year she gives us a progress report on developments at the farm. Plantings have been designed with a warming climate in mind; the system of solar and micro-hydro sources is set up to feed energy back into the grid. In the main house there are facilities for bulk food preservation and storage. I have walked around the site with Amy, marveling at the care and foresight to so many details. Amy describes the vision of living close to the land on what it produces. She grounds this vision solidly in ecological principles, looking clear-eyed at a warming planet. She doesn't exhort the students, she just shares what she knows about sustainable practices and how to plan for a green future. It is obvious that she is extending an invitation to the green lifeway to everyone in the room. Afterward the students come down and mob her with questions, eager to learn more.

If you find you are revising your priorities to reflect your environmental concerns and seeking out friendships that support your environmental priorities, you may see that something significant has shifted in your depth of commitment. Thinking about the earth is no longer something you do now and then; it has become a way of life. Non-harming and systems thinking have become second nature to you. In every situation you look for the green alternative that makes the most environmental sense. Because this is a way of life, you feel morally obliged to look at every aspect of your food choices, your buying patterns, your energy use, your civic contributions to greening your community.

There is no single lifeway to hold up conveniently as a gold standard. You do not necessarily have to be a vegan or vegetarian, or live off-grid or in a green-built house, or have a job influencing environmental policy. You do not have to drive a hybrid car, grow a garden, or wear organic clothing. What marks the green lifeway is not specific choices but depth of commitment and intention. The person in this stage of the practice path takes it very seriously, questioning the impacts of their actions in all that they do. This process of ethical reflection is fueled by a deep and abiding love for the well-being of life on Earth.

From this perspective, any aspect of human activity is open to ethical reflection and incorporation into a green lifeway. In new and inspiring ways, people are carrying this process forward into uncharted territory. Churches and temples are trying to green their sanctuaries as part of their congregational lifeway. Universities are looking for ways to green not only their curricula but also their buildings. A local green parenting store opened up recently on our downtown pedestrian marketplace. Green marriages have come into fashion to support couples committed to caring for the earth in all they do. And there is now a green burial movement in the United States which considers the environmental ethics of our choices in dealing with the dead.

But let me repeat again, lifeway is not lifestyle. It is not about personal choice as a green consumer or the perfecting of green virtue. A lifeway is informed by the wisdom and experience of others and is nourished by building community with others on the green practice path. These may be friends, colleagues, family members, or role models from afar. "Community" may not necessarily mean neighborhood; people following this path find each other across the continent and globe. We encourage each other, we lean on each other, and we build on each other's strengths and experiments. When there are setbacks or frustrations, as in the eight years under President Bush's leadership, we look to others in Europe, India, Australia, and beyond to keep the momentum going and the practice path strong. Experimental communities in places such as Auroville, India, model visions of the future where practicing a green lifeway is backed by infrastructure as well as intention.

Some time ago I came to the realization that no matter how committed I was to a green lifeway, this work would not be completed in my lifetime. The forests would not all grow back, the energy grids would not all go solar, the roads would not all have bike lanes before I left this world. At the time I thought that was discouraging, but mostly it was deeply sobering. It led me to see that it is very important that I pass the green spark on to the next generation. Young people need to be mentored and encouraged to explore the green path of practice. They need support, opportunities, friends, and a multigenerational community of practice partners. The vision I carry of a healthy and life-sustaining earth will take some time to accomplish. It is a cross-generational and cross-cultural project. We don't know how long we must invest in this path of practice. A very important part of following the green lifeway is inviting younger people along, showing them it is possible to nurture the green heart and live a life of conscious intention.

HOW THEN SHALL WE LIVE?

In today's world, the pace of change seems to accelerate exponentially year to year. It is not easy to take the time to reflect on our actions, assess priorities, set intention, and build community. Mostly we fall short of our green hopes and ideals. Sometimes the rate of destruction seems to be speeding up right before our eyes. But it is also true that the rate of learning—the spread of information and new ways of doing things—is faster than we ever could have imagined ten or twenty years ago. Yes, people and nations vary considerably in their commitment to the new sustainability practices. But the overall momentum toward the green practice path is accelerating and headed in the right direction, urged on now by the most pressing matter of climate change.

I know only some pieces of what will be required in taking up these challenges. But I do know we need each others' voices and hearts as we deliberate about how to proceed. The green practice path will be fraught with difficulty; the obstacles are everywhere. We need to understand that these very obstacles are the path. We will all be called to deepen our green commitment to be ready for the complexities, the impossibilities, the world as we can't yet imagine it—both terrible and beautiful in its unfolding.

5

Engaging Skillful Effort

AS WE TAKE UP the green practice path, we begin to see the hurdles before us. Even if we feel confident that we are taking the right steps, we inevitably encounter obstructions and setbacks as we pursue our environmental work. In some countries, a person can be put in jail for speaking out about environmental concerns. Wangari Maathai, the winner of the 2004 Nobel Peace Prize, was beaten and publicly humiliated for her tree-planting campaigns in Kenya. Nigerian activist Ken Saro-Wiwa, whose tribal lands had been abused by oil extraction, was executed with eight others for speaking out on behalf of the Ogoni people. Holding to green principles lays the foundation for the green practice path. This chapter takes up the personal challenges that will test your commitment. It is hard to face these things. We wish they didn't exist. But understanding these challenges is central to the spiritual work of the green practice path.

DIFFICULT MIND STATES

Environmental despair was first identified in the 1960s when people were grappling with the issues raised by the use of nuclear power and the long-term challenges of nuclear waste. The risk of serious exposure to radiation seemed to be very high, whether from plant meltdowns, transportation accidents, or faulty storage. Antinuclear activists found it difficult to arouse the average person on the street to the same levels of concern they were feeling. And worse, they found that over time, they couldn't keep *themselves* aroused to the same degree of heightened anxiety. What was going on? Psychologist Robert J. Lifton, who studied the impacts of Hiroshima on survivors, described a process he called "psychic numbing." This numbing generates a state of dullness—reduced response to life, a short-circuiting of strong feeling, something that happens when we get too scared, too anxious, too concerned, too anything that we can't sustain over time. Something inside us shuts down in a protective way. Enough is enough, the mind says. Don't tell me about one more bad thing.

Fear of strong emotions, fear of feeling guilty or powerless, fear of distressing others—these all prevent people from responding to environmental abuse. We don't know what to do with the feelings that rise up strongly as we hear about another massive oil spill, another round of clear-cutting. These compromised responses are socially reinforced by the apathy of the media and by personal pressures of work and family. Often we feel there is no time to do anything extra, let alone add to our already long list of worries. It is all too easy to settle for political passivity, cynical blaming, or distraction through entertainment. If we feel overwhelmed, it is tempting to just turn away from it all or find a way to escape the bad feelings.

It can seem like the obstacles associated with environmental concerns are different from anything we've seen in the past, somehow more life-threatening, more challenging, more impossible to address. But human societies have faced overwhelming horrors in other centuries that also seemed way beyond anyone's capacities at the time. Bubonic plague, colonization and genocide, the cruelty of slavery, worldwide war—all these have seemed unsurmountable. And yet people have, in fact, taken up very difficult situations and found ways to respond. The environmental work of the twenty-first century is yet another daunting test that will stretch us in ways we can't even begin to imagine. Learning how to carry on environmental work in the company of obstacles will be an important strength to cultivate for the long effort ahead. This chapter takes up the practice of understanding obstacles as not only inevitable but a necessary part of the green path.

We can begin this practice by learning to recognize difficult mind states when they arise and by studying how they affect us personally. The self-help bookshelves offer many guides to understanding the psychology of emotions; I am going to draw on a Buddhist framework because that is the perspective that makes the most sense to me. So far at least, it seems to address the wide range of mind states I've encountered across my years of environmental work. Buddhist psychology is also complementary and supportive of other approaches to emotional awareness. Moreover, Buddhist psychology takes these mind states seriously as a crucial part of the practice path, providing skillful means for working with them. Working directly with difficult emotions can provide a useful grounding in the midst of challenging environmental work.

In a fundamental sense, all feeling states can be described as primarily pleasant, unpleasant, or neutral. Being on a wooded mountain trail breathing fresh air awakens pleasant feelings; driving by an oil refinery spewing smoke awakens unpleasant feelings. The pleasant feelings are attracting; they pull us toward the thing that has stimulated those feelings. The unpleasant feelings are repulsing; they push us away from the stimulating thing or thought. Given a choice, we generally want more of the good feelings and less of the bad feelings. These impulses toward and away are hardwired into our animal bodies, based on the need to find food and mates and to escape predators and other dangers. Neutral feelings pull us neither way, as when we feel confused or unable to take action.

The problem with any of these feelings, from a Buddhist perspective, is identifying with them as part of your personal story, or becoming conditioned by certain emotional habits. Being hooked by feelings happens when we identify with our opinions, our preferences, our desires and appetites, and insist on their rightness. People get hooked by environmentally generated feelings in a number of ways. Some people are caught by a self-righteous sense of virtue or idealism in their concerns; some are hooked by alarmist fears of nuclear meltdown or climate catastrophe that keep them awake at night. Being "hooked" means being stuck, obsessed, caught, and generally unable to see the feeling as a passing phenomenon.

Buddhist teachers speak of the "three poisons"—greed, hate, and delusion—as the feelings that most disturb the mind. Named in such strong terms, you might not relate to them—who wants to think of themselves as greedy, hateful, or deluded? The three poisons are shorthand terms for the three tendencies related to our feelings—to go toward what we want (greed), to turn away from what we don't want (hate, or aversion), and to be confused by what we don't understand (delusion). Environmental debates are often marked by strong rhetoric of blame and aversion, pointing to the destructive horrors of modern industrialism. They can also be quite deluded by dreams of back-to-the-land simplicity, which overlook gaping class and race differences. The challenge of the green practice path is to be aware of these feelings and watch how they work in the mind, even though this may be uncomfortable and even painful at times.

We could make a list of the most wearing mind states that seem to undermine our intentions and best efforts for environmental progress. Here are some that have ravaged my own attention at different times: Fear of a frightening future, with destructive climate events or deathly pandemics. Anger at those who block citizen initiatives for clean energy or global cooperation. Despair for the damaged world our children will inhabit. Worry that not enough can be done fast enough. Grief for the hundreds of species and beautiful places being lost or degraded beyond repair. Cynicism and exhaustion—will anything we do really matter against the dominant political forces? Ignorance and helplessness in seeing our own limits of knowledge and power. These are powerful mind states.

By focusing our attention on the experience of the feelings, we can keep from being swept away by them. By staying present in the actual moment of the troublesome mind state, we engage it directly and can observe how it affects us. The goal in this practice is to conserve energy—our own energy, that is. We want to minimize the loss of energy to mind states that distract and drain us, because we need all the energy we can generate to address the environmental dilemmas before us. We can't afford to spend weeks or months lost in despair or anxiety.

Buddhist psychology speaks of the "five hindrances" to a calm mind, flames of strong feeling and mental unrest that can be cooled by the practice of mindfulness. These are: greed, ill will, dullness or sleepiness, worry and anxiety, and doubt. The first one, greed, is said to be like a trap that keeps us in its hold—wanting things to be different, wanting more knowledge before we act, or wanting more people to support our ideas. These traps hold us back from being present with how things actually are. Anger or ill will is more like a sickness that eats away inside of you. It might take the form of resentment or blame against those who are causing environmental damage. We think, *It is all their fault*—they are the ones who are destroying the forests, polluting our drinking water. But this anger is like boiling water; it scalds you more than anyone else, for you are the pot, boiling over with rage.

Drowsiness comes on us when we are exhausted from our emotional struggles. We may feel some respite and relief from the endless battles, but then may feel sleepy and be unable to concentrate. Dullness overcomes the sluggish mind, weary from too many e-mails, too many opinions, too many things to do. The mind loses its flexibility and vitality, worn down and unable to respond. Worry and anxiety work in the opposite way, overstimulating the mind. We get hooked on our own adrenaline, afraid that if we stop worrying we won't be able to keep going with the tasks before us. This hindrance is sometimes compared to slavery; we become enslaved to our worries for the planet and can never enjoy peace of mind.

Doubt, like all the other hindrances, comes up regularly in addressing environmental issues. In many situations, we really do not know what the next step is or what the right thing is to do. We are having to invent responses to situations we have never seen before. It is very easy to begin doubting yourself and your capacities; you can feel lost and without direction. Your inner voice might needle you: *You're not smart enough to handle this,* or *You're not spiritual enough—who do you think you are?* This can be very unsettling, particularly for someone who is used to passionately following their environmental ideals. Doubt sows confusion and makes it hard to move actions forward. Doubting others and doubting oneself both undermine progress, leaving the situation dangling and unresolved.

How then, do we learn to "be with" these difficult mind states? How do we learn to practice with these obstacles without being swept away by their power? The first step is naming the mind states as they arise. Some people practice this naming in the quiet space of meditation. But you do not have to meditate to be aware of these obstacles; they will present themselves for your attention if you are alert. In the midst of a public hearing or a political showdown, you can pause and ask yourself: *What am I feeling now? What is going on here? How am I being hooked by this feeling? How is it affecting my behavior?* As you take the time to be with the feelings, you gain familiarity with your own emotional triggers around environmental concerns. This helps you contain your emotional heat and leave more space for others in the conversation. As you focus on the awareness rather than on the passion of the feelings, you cultivate equanimity and mental stability for more challenges ahead.

WORKING WITH THE OBSTACLES

What might this practice look like if we apply it to a difficult environmental concern? I'll nominate climate change, because that is the one I am wrestling with right now myself. And I'm hardly alone. My college president and state governor are wrestling with it. My senators and representatives are wrestling with it. And my young students, barely into their twenties, are trying to figure out how to cope with something that will rearrange their entire world. I think it is highly likely that we will run into many, if not all, of these challenging mind states as we turn to face the all-encompassing all-hands-on-deck situation of climate change. I confess there are days I want to escape into denial and days I just wring my hands with worry. Watching the arctic ice shrink beyond anyone's projections certainly doesn't help.

Let's consider three practice approaches as possible ways to work with the obstacles of climate change. Buddhist environmental teacher and activist Joanna Macy has developed a process that works with emotions as bound energy, capable of transformation.[1] Originally called "despair and empowerment work," her guided exercises help people acknowledge their pain for the suffering of the world under assault. Through simple questioning, listening, and instructed activity, people are invited to express what they have been feeling—the fear, grief, guilt, helplessness. I have participated in a number of workshops with Joanna and taken her advanced trainings, eventually facilitating the work in my own teaching. I consider Joanna to be a primary mentor in shaping my sense of how important it is to address deeply held environmental concerns. I was carrying no small measure of despair and worry for our world when I first learned of this work. Macy encourages people to see that strong feelings are a compassionate response to the world, a form of energy that can be freed up for constructive action.

When we express our feelings as honestly and clearly as we can, we arrive fully in the present moment, accepting that "this is how it is right now." We can then take the next step of reconsidering our usual self-absorbed perspective by shifting to a systems view. We do this through a shift of focus, away from our immediate pain and toward the big-system energy flows we are participating in all the time. We see ourselves as part of those flows, with momentum and opportunity. This new perspective generates a natural transformation from bound pain to unbound creativity. The process can be experienced in one of Macy's exercises that is based on the Tibetan meditation practice of *tonglen*. This practice is a way of both being with the difficult emotions and also transforming them into generative energy.

We can try this out with climate change. We begin by tuning in to the breath, to the ribbon of air that moves through the nose, into the chest and abdomen, visualizing the breath-stream as it moves in and out, connecting us with the larger web of life. Then we imagine in our minds' eye the hardships we know already that are a part of climate change . . . flooding in New Orleans from Hurricane Katrina, melting ice in Greenland, polar bears threatened with extinction, coral reefs bleaching in overheated water. Worry arises, we breathe through. We call to mind the harsh droughts of summer and parched fields of corn. Despair arises, we breathe through. We think of island peoples driven from their homes as the ocean floods the shore. Fear arises, we breathe through.

As we breathe, we stay present with ourselves. We pay attention while the waves of feeling present themselves, while we observe the difficult mind states. When a wave of feeling subsides, we return to the stabilizing breath, the sense of being connected with the wider web of life. As Macy says, we allow ourselves to "be breathed by life;"[2] we trust the wider web to support us and help transform the difficult mind states. Grief arises, the breath tightens. Breathing through to connection, the breath relaxes. The breath becomes a direct aid to both observing and letting go of obstacles. For Macy, trained in the Tibetan Buddhist tradition, this practice is a foundation for envisioning a more sustainable world, literally available through freeing the mind.

The Tibetan approach and Macy's creative imagination were, for me, a stark contrast to the spare contours of Zen practice, my own root training. The Zen way is not for everyone, but it has a sharp clarity that can be very effective in practicing with difficult mind states. Formal Zen centers often have a statue of Manjusri on the altar as a reminder to students of his power to "cut through." Manjusri is the bodhisattva of wisdom, and he is usually depicted holding a sword in one hand, ready to cut through delusion and attachment. Students are encouraged to use the sword with their own minds, cutting through the debilitating effects of the hindrances. Like the famous "whack!" of the stick, this method is firm and direct, no nonsense. It can appear harsh, but in fact it is refreshing to be liberated from the paralysis of certain mind states. Suddenly there is the bigger truth in front of you, the whole situation, the big energetic dynamic playing through of all the parts. And "whack!" Your own self-absorption in fear or grief has evaporated.

How might that work for the person concerned with climate change? I find myself groaning as I prepare my class lecture on climate change, putting together the facts and figures of a planet under assault. The experts say we have only ten years to turn this around. I have read the books and reports. I know too much. I am awash in concern. Will there be a pandemic from some new pathogen that has surged into new habitat? Will there be terrible wars for the last remaining oil reserves? What horrors will my students witness? I am sinking, I am anxious, how can I talk about this with them? *Whack, whack! Get out the sword! Stop before you drown!* The mind clears, just enough to consider: *Hey! There might be something else happening besides my feelings!* I remember the students are organizing for a big event near Washington, D.C.—the first national youth summit on climate change. How can I invest my energy in that? Creativity is flowing now, I contact the organizer, invite her to class to tell everyone what's happening. I will invite those who are going to the conference to come down in front so we can invest our class energy in them. And then, I think, let's pass the hat for them! And I will pledge to get our faculty to match whatever the students throw in.

What happened here? The terrible projections of the future were clogging my mind with debilitating feeling states. I didn't stop to analyze them, name them, or even focus my breathing on them. I just got out the sword and cut them off. Radical! And refreshing. Something moved, my self-centered views dropped away. I realized there were other people in the picture; I could put my energy into them instead of my feeling states. It changed my orientation to climate change; I could be part of what the young people were doing. For them, this is an unprecedented opportunity to create a better world than the one they've inherited. Let's go with that; I'll keep that Manjusri sword handy for the next round of anxiety.

Both of these approaches may not be easily accessible without some training. The third approach, however, is based on straightforward common sense, drawn from the earliest Buddhist teachings on skillful effort. "Effort," in this context, means firm resolve to address difficult mind states and minimize their impact. "Skillful" means using an approach that is effective and reliable. Skillful effort is another one of the eight spokes of practice that the Buddha taught in his Four Noble Truths. He offered it as a way to address everyday mental and emotional suffering. I believe this approach can also work for the mind states we experience as we think about climate change.

There are four steps in this approach; these should be thought of as long-term reorientation in working with feelings that affect our capacity to do good environmental work.[3] The first step is to *prevent negative states of mind* from arising. This requires vigilant mindfulness practice and intimate familiarity with our own tendencies and hooks. People working with climate change report some of these common mind states: anger at the slow pace of government action, frustration at trying to communicate technical information, alarm at the spread of pests with the warming climate. Negative mind states are those that spiral downward into hopelessness, choking off a wider view of the dynamics in motion. They arise from dwelling on the emotion, investing in it, using it to alarm others or to generate urgency that will motivate action. But that absorption detracts from establishing a peaceful and flexible mind.

What to do then? You use mindfulness to return to the present moment, to the realities before you and see, for example, *Ah! I'm feeling discouraged today about my government's resistance to the science of global warming.* Stop right there: *I'm feeling discouraged.* You watch that mind state as it is contained in your experience, you stay with it while the feeling is strong, and then you remember, *I am not the whole world!* As I tell my students, we need to remind ourselves that other countries are taking significant steps to manage carbon emissions; they are not waiting for us. The United Kingdom is working toward target goals for reducing emissions; Germany has built acres of wind farms; Japan is developing affordable solar technology. It is important to remember that your own discouragement is not stopping the world from moving forward; it is just what you are feeling at the moment.

You can watch how certain hooks set you up for negative mind states—for example, watching the news on television just before bed. Sometimes stress at work or at home leaves you vulnerable to difficult emotions regarding the environment. Many people are more prone to negative mind states under the influence of biochemical body states induced by alcohol, drugs, sugar, lack of sleep, or no exercise. The Buddha warned his students to learn to endure small irritations. In today's society we are used to adjusting everything to our exact liking; we are hooked on our own needs for comfort and control. This can get in the way of applying skillful effort where it is needed.

The second step is *overcoming negative mind states* after they have arisen. Once a hindrance has gotten a toehold in your mind, it can be hard to dislodge. You might be sunk in depression (sluggishness) or burning with rage toward "the system." Rather than thinking these feelings will just go away in time, it is more effective to give them your complete attention and see what you can find out. You can begin to notice how the feeling state is blocking your equanimity, how it is causing you mental or even physical harm as it persists. You can look closely to see the multiple causes that are contributing to the mind state. You can remind yourself that nothing lasts forever, whatever you fear about climate change. The hardest mind states to overcome are those that are deeply entrenched. It may be necessary to be more firm or disciplined with yourself, making a strong effort to corral your energy for more productive activity. You reaffirm your recommitment to the practice path, remembering we need all our bright minds and good energy to tackle the frightening implications of climate change.

The third step is to *cultivate positive states of mind*. By "positive," I mean healthy, relaxed, able to function, content. It seems that many people are often more inclined to generate negative states of mind than positive states. But if you take up this practice, you will see immediate benefits. It is possible to intentionally bring up positive states of mind such as compassion for others' suffering, joy in others' accomplishments, stabilizing equanimity, and kindness toward others. For some people, this takes the form of prayer, an active invocation for the well-being of all. In systems thinking, we would say that these mind states generate positive or amplifying feedback, bringing more kindness, more equanimity, more joy, and more compassion into a situation fraught with obstacles. Bringing these qualities to climate change discussions can reduce conflict and encourage more people to feel welcome to share their ideas.

The fourth step is to *maintain positive states of mind*. The better you get at recognizing difficult mind states and overcoming them, the more you will be able to cultivate and maintain positive mind states. Calm and good-spirited mind states are attractive to others; they encourage people to want to work with you on a common project.

Positive states of mind make it much more possible to take up challenges as comprehensive as climate change. This is deep personal work that carries through to more than just environmental challenges. It is a matter of spiritual discipline to take good care of a positive state of mind. You could say that climate change work rests on maintaining a positive *mental* climate, a flexible and resilient mind that rejoices in the vitality of life. Imagine such a positive mental climate pervading negotiations on climate change. Under the influence of calm and good-spirited mind states, people might be more willing to drop their individual agendas to work for the positive benefit of all. The benefits of spiritual practice can very quickly bring tangible and practical results.

AN ETHIC OF RESTRAINT

Many moments of skillful effort on the green practice path add up to a lifetime practice of mindfulness. Ethical and spiritual engagement offers tremendous support for environmental work. His Holiness the Dalai Lama recommends cultivating a habit of inner discipline. In his book, *Ethics for the New Millennium* (1999), he points out that lack of inner restraint is the source of unethical conduct. Inner discipline is a voluntary and intentional effort exemplified in the practice of skillful effort. Such an effort is not about choosing a specific religion or being part of a religious community. It is about ethical actions and inner discipline as they help us become effective environmental citizens. Working with difficult mind states is part of the practice of inner discipline and carries long-term developmental consequences. We can use this work to become not just better advocates for the environment but kinder human beings.

In this context, we can see it is not only useful but perhaps one of the best things we can do to take difficult mind states seriously. People bring their emotional habits and histories with them into their environmental work. If they see themselves as victims, they will look for people to blame for environmental suffering. If they are used to having everything their way in every decision, they will be poorly equipped to listen to people with different views. Most of us are fairly blind to the emotional and cultural habits that drive us. It is not unusual for someone to replay their family-of-origin dramas in the setting of a small environmental nonprofit organization.

A strong motivation for many of us who take up environmental work is our sense that people have acted unethically toward the land, the animals, the beloved places, the earth as a whole. People in the environmental movement often suggest that we need better social ethics if we are to sustain our economies, governments, families, and communities into the future. What needs changing, they say, is not just the polluted air and water but the ethics that permitted the pollution in the first place. Environmental philosophers have proposed many guidelines for ethical relations with all beings. We have much to draw on here, from Aldo Leopold's land ethic to the Dalai Lama's ethic of universal responsibility. These ideas and many others are part of an evolving social ethic regarding our environmental relations. As environmental concerns mount, it becomes imperative that we change our fundamental approach to the earth.

But we can't simply take a position and tell other people to change. It is much more effective in the long run to model the ethical behavior we wish to promote. This requires taking up our own ethical work with wholehearted commitment. By being more honest with ourselves, we are less likely to project our unconscious feelings onto others. By dealing with our own difficult mind states, we come to understand that all human beings must grapple with these things; it is very much what makes us human. Working with the obstacles can become a way of connecting with others, offering kindness to soften the challenges of the green practice path.

6

Seeking Wisdom Sources

ONCE YOU TAKE UP THE GREEN PRACTICE PATH, you see that environmental caregiving is a lifelong task. The changes that need to happen may even take generations. We absolutely cannot do this work alone. We need the encouragement and inspiration of others. We need the guidance of those ahead of us on the path, those with green wisdom who can help us find our way. These wisdom sources can strengthen our practice commitment and challenge us to go further. They can demonstrate ethical integrity for us to emulate. They can help us remember that others have taken up this work before us and made it possible for us to do the piece we are doing now. The green practice path is a long road with many kind beings along the way. Just as the obstacles are everywhere, so too are the teachers. They appear as we need them; we bring them forward with our calls for help. And we, too, in whatever stage of the green path, can be wisdom sources for others, passing the green spark along.

SEEKING WISDOM FROM OTHERS

When I was in junior high school I stumbled on a book by Joseph Wood Krutch called *The Great Chain of Being*. I didn't really know what

I'd found; it was just another volume from the school library that looked interesting. As a young teen I read constantly, seeking solace in words and privacy from my rowdy family. Something about the spare, poetic language of this naturalist caught my attention. Krutch wrote with a gentle authority, based on hours of field observations, watching the desert rhythms and web of life. His stories revealed the grand beauty of life, the wholeness of nature. He was saying something very important that I had not yet run into in science class or church or listening to my parents. Though I was barely an adolescent at the time, I believe this was my first taste of green wisdom-seeking mind.

After I graduated from college, in the early days of the environmental movement, that love of nature was turned upside down with agonizing questions. Why were we killing the remarkable giants of the sea, the gentle blue whales? Why were we spraying dangerous toxins on the land? What would really happen if the earth's population doubled? And scariest of all, what about nuclear radiation? I, like many others, was desperate for thoughtful reflection on these difficult topics. I looked to Rachel Carson, Barry Commoner, Paul Ehrlich—the few lone scientists speaking out about the serious implications of ecological disaster. Maybe they could provide guidance in finding a wise path forward.

Still seeking wisdom, I returned to Krutch and discovered that he drew his philosophy from Albert Schweitzer, the German theologian who served as a medical missionary to Africa in the early twentieth century. Schweitzer's selfless work and guiding philosophy earned him the 1952 Nobel Peace Prize. His book, *Out of My Life and Thought* (1931), offered me a grounding point as I tried to find my way through the environmental crisis.[1] Schweitzer called his philosophy "reverence for life"—a recognition that all life is sacred and "unfathomably mysterious." Understanding this central truth, the moral person should act to preserve and protect life. This made complete sense to me; I could not stand to squash a ladybug nor see my country at war. Schweitzer demonstrated that it was not only possible but deeply satisfying to live by this philosophy.

Root teachers such as Schweitzer are cultural transmitters of life-giving environmental values. Tapping into their wisdom streams can provide a well of energy and insight as we take up the great unknowns of environmental work. We cannot come up with all the answers on our own. Following these issues over many years, I see that it is not uncommon for those engaging environmental concerns to be seeking wisdom sources of one form or another. They have lifted up the ecological wisdom in writings by Henry David Thoreau and John Muir. They have found insight in nature writing such as Annie Dillard's *Pilgrim at Tinker Creek* and Edward Abbey's *Desert Solitaire*. Indigenous people, ecofeminists, and environmental justice advocates have contributed their perspectives based on alternate ways of knowing. And now an increasing number of people are drawing on world religions, seeking ecological guidance from ancient wisdom traditions. This seeking seems to be a natural corollary to environmental work, arising because we find ourselves in such uncharted territory and greatly in need of guidance.

As a teacher myself, I am interested in how people seek out teachers and what they consider to be key learning experiences. I ask my students to write an environmental autobiography, naming key events and people, telling the stories of their environmental awakenings. Sometimes the teachers are parents or ministers; sometimes they are animal members of the family or beloved trees. It might be a particular place that carries meaning, revealing its natural wisdom over time. By asking students to articulate these forms of transmission, I am intentionally encouraging wisdom-seeking mind. I want them to value their own learning experiences and recognize those who have given them teachings along the path. I see them feeling overwhelmed by the fears of climate change and peak oil or the monster of consumerism, and I remember my own frightened loneliness in the face of it all. But now I know there are teachers everywhere, available for the seeking, and I want my students to waste no time in finding green wisdom.

THE SEEKING PROCESS

How do you look for a teacher or wisdom source? What does it mean in spiritual traditions to take up the "way-seeking mind"? It seems that finding wisdom happens in as many ways as there are people. Often it starts with the simple request for help. There are at least two broad approaches to finding guidance along the green practice path. One is systematic, the other serendipitous. The systematic seeker is methodical in finding resources or direction along their environmental path. They make appointments with advisers, they plan their courses of action carefully, they engage the structures of learning to see what they can offer. They may read widely but purposefully, looking for the bright minds in their area of interest. They investigate organizations on the internet, looking for a good fit with their values. Systematic seekers often have strong focus or intention and are able to comb through many potential resources in the hopes of finding a guiding framework or insightful mind.

Serendipitous seekers, on the other hand, usually have only a general sense of where they're headed or maybe no plan at all in mind. They have great faith that life will turn up what they need. If there is a long dry spell, that is all part of the process. This approach is more like following a meandering stream that keeps shifting course. The serendipitous seeker is content with each stop along the way that supplies adequate resources, nourishing the traveler to continue with the journey. This works best when the seeker comes with open hands and a willingness to learn from what presents itself. You might think of the long-distance backpacker, following a trail or landform, and figuring it out as he or she goes along. Wisdom could arrive in the form of unexpected shelter, enlightening company, or insight from a ridge-top landmark.

Most people experience a mix of these two approaches, depending on their changing life circumstances and what suits their personalities. If the faith approach is not turning up much wisdom, then it may be time to take up the systematic approach. If the systematic approach starts to feel like a straitjacket, then it is time to break the mold and go off in a new direction. Seeking wisdom sources for environmental work is a personal process; it might be motivated by professional ambition or moral angst. It might be addressing a need for support or a need for stimulation. Each person's journey is unique; each person has their own wisdom-seeking story to uncover. So much depends on the nature of the need, the intensity of the seeking, the character of the seeker. Sometimes an inspiring environmental writer such as Barry Lopez or Gretel Ehrlich can offer poetic insight for direction. Sometimes a thoughtful conversation, one on one, with a potential mentor in the field provides needed encouragement. Other times it is best to just go for a walk and listen to the trees.

Both types of seeking can be enhanced by using systems thinking. It is crucial to see yourself as part of an open system of wisdom transmission, flowing across time through generations and across space through networks of communication. If you are feeling the isolation of environmental despair or the sag of helplessness, it may require effort to take up a different perspective. Sensing this flow of wisdom is a way of making yourself available to it, even in a not-yet-manifest way. From here it is possible to sharpen your sensors for positive and negative feedback, using even the most subtle signals as directional cues. If you were using systematic seeking, for example, you might attend a number of talks on the environment by expert speakers. At each talk, you could be paying close attention to your responses, listening to your internal comments saying, *Yes, yes, tell me more* (positive flow-enhancing feedback), or *No, that's not it* (negative flow-dampening feedback). "No, that's not it" does not necessarily mean you are critical of the speaker; it may just be that this person or this information is not an appropriate wisdom source for you right now with your particular questions. "Yes, yes, tell me more" tells you this is a direction to pursue, to see what it can yield.

It is also possible to test this feedback or set up criteria that can help with the discernment process. Because so many of today's environmental problems carry a moral dimension, it is important to look for teachers whose ethics are consistent with their actions. One of my first socially engaged Buddhist teachers, Robert Aiken of Hawaii, inspired me with his commitment to war tax resistance. As a young man, Aiken had spent some formative years in the Philippines during World War II, so he knew something of the personal anguish of war. Because of his Buddhist vows of non-harming, he felt he could not support the violence and killing of war in any way. So every year he refused to pay income taxes as part of the antiwar effort. Aiken knew the jarring impact of war on the environment. He encouraged his students to take up environmental concerns, applying the principles of the Buddhist precepts. In his teaching, Aiken shared his own deep love for the natural world, drawing on the precepts as a guide for appropriate action. I listened to his words, but I was even more impressed to see how strongly his ethical integrity manifested in his actions.

For some people, the wisdom-seeking process follows emotional response, a felt sense that the wisdom teacher is "on your wavelength" in speaking about shared concerns. When Terry Tempest Williams published her first book, *Refuge,* many readers found emotional resonance with her expressions of concern. She told the story of her family exposure to nuclear testing in the Utah desert and how breast cancer showed up in generation after generation of her female relatives. Paralleling this story was a chronicle of threats to Great Salt Lake, impacting her much-beloved waterbirds. Williams wrote in such personal terms that readers relived the story with her and saw immediately the links between human and environmental health and how both love and tragedy could penetrate your family. Through this award-winning book, Williams validated for many the powerful role of emotions in responding to environmental abuse.

Wisdom has perennially been associated with ethics; some green wisdom teachers have articulated environmental ethics that provide ideological frameworks for environmental action. Arne Naess, a Norwegian philosopher and activist, developed the ideas that became known as "deep ecology," providing an alternative to the mainstream view, which he called "shallow ecology."[2] As a climber and mountaineer as well as a professor, Naess drew attention to hydropower plans that would dam waterfalls and destroy Norway's beautiful fjords. He was among the first to place himself in harm's way to draw attention to threatened places. His philosophy derived directly from personal experience, what he described as *self-realization through ecological identification* with other beings. Naess maintained that the most convincing environmental ethics rest on experiential insights of relationship with other life-forms that expand one's own sense of self. From his deep ecology perspective, all beings are potential wisdom sources in the wide web of life.

SEEING TEACHERS EVERYWHERE

Twenty years ago I enrolled in a seminary program to explore my own need for wisdom sources and my desire to consider a professional career in the ministry. One course was a private tutorial on the Gospels of Jesus, introduced by reading Martin Buber's *I and Thou*. Each week the professor would clear his desk, light a small candle, and invite me to consider the "green circuitry" of meaning that flowed from what I was reading. He was presenting a koan about love as expressed by Martin Buber and Jesus, and I sought a way to enter it that made sense to me. I wondered aloud to him if Jesus loved trees as Buber did. I wanted to spend time with trees and ask that question in their presence, to see what could happen if you approached trees as wisdom sources. It seemed like a heretical idea considering the history of Christian attacks on paganism, but the professor encouraged me. He had his own relationship with a towering maple in his yard and felt my questions were valid.

During that semester I wrote three short pieces in my journal, undertaking tutelage at the foot of several trees that called to me. I didn't really know what I was doing, but I tried my best not to "channel" messages or make up anthropomorphic responses. To "hear" the trees, I had to clear my mind as best I could of human projection. In this, my Zen practice was very helpful, although I struggled with expressing my experience in human language. My classmates encouraged me to continue the experiment, and soon I found myself seeking out a number of trees I had met over my time in California. I never knew what would come from these meetings, but always there was a story. On one outing in winter I felt called to visit the coast redwoods down in the creek near my house. When it started to rain, I sought shelter in the stump of an ancient old-growth tree, cut perhaps a hundred years ago and charred on the inside from passing fires. There were many striking trees all around me, but I stayed with the old tree, stretching my mind back into the history of redwood decimation. I tried to listen to the whole story—logging camps, settling the west, rebuilding San Francisco, protecting the remaining giants. Tears of sorrow streamed down my face in the rain, even as I acknowledged the new trees sprouting from the old ones' stumps. The visits to trees turned into a life journey, and in the end I had written twenty-seven stories, each a different encounter yielding unexpected gifts of wisdom. They became a book (*The Attentive Heart: Conversations with Trees*), and when I gave readings, I found people eager to share their tree experiences with me for validation from a kindred spirit. I realized I had tapped into an ancient stream of tree wisdom-seeking, deep in my own druidic Celtic European roots.

Animals, like trees, can also be wisdom teachers. My students describe close relations with companion animals, sensing their empathy and lived wisdom in some unspoken way. Native peoples living closely with the natural world understand animals to be kindred spirits. For centuries various clans and tribes have aligned themselves with the spirit of Bear, Coyote, Wolf, or Salmon. Through chants and stories, the teachings of the wisdom guides are kept alive in the culture. In my own early years as an environmentalist, I felt called to work on behalf of the great whales, sensing a wisdom power in these animals that should be protected. To come up right next to a gray whale in the calving lagoon and touch its skin was a life-altering experience for me. I wanted everyone to have this opportunity to be so close to such remarkable beings.

To call forth the wisdom teachings of animals, the Australian activist John Seed developed an experiential process that he called the Council of All Beings.[3] In these ritual workshops, council participants spend solo time seeking the guidance of a mentor from the natural world and then return to share the wisdom with the council circle. They temporarily assume the identity of their mentor (owl, snake, tree, moon) and speak from a different perspective. Later they resume their human identity and receive the gifts of the mentor, offering gratitude for the teachings. Thousands of people around the world have undertaken these councils and found significant insight from accessing animal wisdom.

Places can be teachers too, carrying the cumulative wisdom of all that has happened over time in a particular location. You can ask yourself: Which places speak most strongly to you? Are you a forest person? A desert person? Are you a lake lover or river watcher? Which places have offered you wisdom and drawn you back again and again? The wisdom places whose smells and sounds offer specific teachings that "fit" for you are the places most deeply entrained in your heart. We don't always know why certain places feel so powerful or alive. As part of the tree journey, I traveled to Tuolumne

Valley in the high country of Yosemite National Park. I wanted to climb Lembert Dome again, both to visit the whitebark pines and to see the valley from this exposed monolith of glacier-scoured granite. The hike took on the air of pilgrimage as I climbed out from the forest onto the wind-blasted dome. The entire dome felt sacred as a landmark to many peoples before me, a geologic testimony to the frozen history of that land. I found my wisdom place on the sheared edge of the dome, looking straight down into big space.

Sacred places have been described by poets, shamans, psychologists, and naturalists. We know each place to be a unique geography of landforms, weather events, and hundreds of criss-crossing paths of people, birds, winds, and insects over time. Specific places hold specific histories whose stories carry meaning from one generation to the next. What makes a place numinous or filled with wisdom energy is more than anyone could ever completely explain, and that mystery itself is a teaching.

Trees, plants, animals, places—I am naming these possibilities to illustrate the many options for green mentoring within the streaming field of wisdom in the great web of life. Zen Buddhists believe that stones and waterfalls are also vibrant with life force and history. A rich Japanese tradition parallel to the art of bonsai has developed around special stones of great energetic immanence (*sui seki*). At the Japanese Garden in Portland, Oregon, there is an arresting garden of seven stones placed in a raked sand field, sixty feet wide and forty feet deep. Every time I visit I want to stop and stay with these stones, listening, sensing: *What are they saying? What is it about how they are placed? Why is it so compelling?* How perfect it is and yet how inscrutable. Nearby a small creek tumbles through, coming to rest in a quiet pool. The light plays on the water, the waves push through each other in endless patterns delighting the eye. These elemental forms of life energy—water and stone—call directly to the source materials from which we are made as human beings. Our limbic resonance is awakened and something big and true comes in. We listen through

our larger selves, we experience "self-realization" as Arne Naess describes, and in tasting this vast stream of life we open to the wisdom
we are seeking.

Particularly strong experiences of this flowing wisdom stream
could be called *epiphanies,* moments of powerful connecting insight
that shift internal understanding to a new configuration. The Greek
roots of the word mean "showing forth, manifestation," a revelation
of the world in a fresh way. Many people working with the environment have had such epiphanies, though most keep them as private
moments, not often shared in public. One story well-known to environmental advocates is Aldo Leopold's dramatic epiphany after he
chased a female wolf into a canyon and took her down.[4] In those
days you shot at any wolf you could see. But as this wolf lay dying,
Leopold looked into her wild green eyes and saw that the wolf was
more than predator. She was mother, ancient one, traveler, a part of
the very mountains he loved. This experience was a significant turning point in Leopold's ecological consciousness. To recall this famous
epiphany, former Earth First! leader Dave Foreman concludes his
talks by inviting his audience to join him in a long group wolf howl.
The experience of an epiphany is different for each person, but it is
often described as spiritual awakening, a sense of being "one" with
the miraculous world and suddenly motivated to care for it with new
fierceness. The experience itself becomes the teacher; the wisdom
flows from full delivery of unexpected insight.

DON'T KNOW MIND

When I first came to the small Zen center in Santa Cruz, I had not
met the teacher and had no idea what to expect. Like most Westerners, my mind was filled with ideas and projections about what a
Zen master was, and I had an appetite for the exotic experience of
meditation. When Kobun Chino walked through the door, I stole a

glance at him from my meditation cushion, wondering what he looked like. He seemed to glide across the floor barely touching the ground, a cloud drifting across the room. How did he do that? I was completely mystified. Perhaps he was trained as a Zen novice to move this way, soundlessly, with empty mind. Perhaps it was his unique style. He seemed to move as if there was no barrier between him and the floor, or anything else for that matter. He was completely open, just arriving to whatever was happening. No separation between him and others. I came to think of his walking as a manifestation of "don't know mind," a way of being present, not holding back, not coming forward.

Cultivating don't know mind takes wisdom-seeking to another level of transformation. There are Zen teachings that reveal something about the teacher; there are teachings that reveal something about the world. Don't know mind teachings reveal the student to the student, opening the door to new worlds of understanding. Most of the time we live within our own proscribed worlds—you could call them "flat" worlds—supported by others and held in place by accepted boundaries. Most of us have great fear of going anywhere beyond the familiar. The teacher who invites us to a more spacious realm is asking us to trust in don't know mind and be willing to see something much more vast.

Is this part of the path of the wisdom-seeking environmentalist? I think so. Environmentalists are very good with ecological surveys, policy analysis, and citizen campaigns, but they can be as blind as anyone absorbed in their own small world. Ideals and passions often make for self-righteous proclamations and aggressive insistence on the environmentally "right" thing to do. Environmentalists have their own version of "flat" worlds, which keep them closed to different viewpoints. The daily frustration of battling with other positions and agendas is wearing; it produces insults and enemies that harden into histories. But there may be another way to approach this work that holds to don't know mind. I might call this the gliding path, the path that perceives no obstacles. Wisdom-seeking is then part of awakening to the Big Dance, everyone part of the grand improvisation, enemies and all. The environmentalist who pursues this path is less interested in anger and retribution and more interested in being present to the whole story. This can have very practical application in the everyday world. A situation can seem completely stuck, no solutions in sight, and then an opening appears in some completely unpredicted way. The practitioner of don't know mind is able to spot the opening and follow it, leaving behind the trappings of defenses and political habit.

Certainly it helps to have a teacher point out the flat worlds that limit us. But physical practices can help too. Consider the patient fly fisherman waiting with no thoughts—what will come of each cast? Or the alert naturalist on a field survey, watching for both the familiar and the unfamiliar. In Buddhist traditions one of the most humbling practices of don't know mind is bowing. Rita Gross, a feminist Buddhist scholar and teacher in the Tibetan lineage, describes her spiritual foundation practice of a hundred thousand prostrations, from full standing to complete floor extension, over and over again across many weeks.[5] She was told to visualize a large tree just beyond a small lake in a grass meadow, with all the gurus of her lineage sitting in the branches of the tree. The bowing was a way of expressing respect for the teachers and gratitude for the teachings, for the very opportunity to receive teachings. From a Western perspective, bowing can seem like a demeaning activity, surrendering to another person, "lowering" yourself, feeling vulnerable. But this is not the point. Bowing is a relational action; it establishes a bond with the teacher and a willingness in the student. Like any practice, it must be taken up and experienced personally for you to know what it actually means. In her own way, forest activist Julia Butterfly Hill was deeply engaged in bowing practice with Luna, the old-growth redwood giant that held her in its branches for two full years. To prevent loggers from cutting down the tree, Julia had set up camp in the redwood's canopy. Friends brought her food under cover of night and helped her communicate her concern for the trees to the world. Bowing to rain, bowing to wind, bowing to loggers, bowing to the strength and wisdom of the old tree itself, bowing to the story as it unfolded, the action became bigger than anything she ever planned.

The ultimate form of don't know mind practice is sitting with death. This is not for the faint of heart. If you are already on the verge of despair over the loss of orangutans or polar bears, or your heart aches with the slaughter of forests, this may be difficult. You might think there has been enough death already, that the world's precious ecosystems can bear no more destruction. Entering into don't know mind may lead you into a bigger picture of death and life. As my mother lay dying from Alzheimer's, taking her last breaths, I thought, *I am sitting at the edge of the gate.* There was great openness there, great don't know mind. I didn't know what would happen, how she would pass over. Instead of feeling scary, it felt incredibly grounding. This was the whole view, the deep view—death as part of life, life passing on into new forms, life and death ever arising. Taking this view can be very settling for the grieving environmentalist, who sees so much being lost on such a planetary scale. It becomes imperative to pass the teachings on, to see yourself as part of the universal flow of vitality, doing your part and helping others who will follow after you.

THE REAL WORK

The wisdom-seeking process is not a single path nor a predictable path. As the Tao Te Ching states: "The way that can be followed is not the constant way." The wisdom way is not a linear road one can hop on like a moving walkway at the airport. The way is open in all directions, no obstacles. It may not be what we think it is. It may not be entered only through discipline or virtue. Some Zen teachers even discourage their students from taking the path too seriously, admonishing them to drop all aspirations. They might say, "Give up trying to make things better, just be your true self." What does this mean? What sort of awakening are we talking about in this wisdom-seeking?

The poet and Zen student Gary Snyder suggests that "the intention of training can only be accomplished when the 'follower' has been forgotten."[6] Wisdom comes from seeing through the constructions of ego that keep us in our flat worlds and from waking up to the infinite universe, which is so much bigger than our small self-perceptions. Letting go of our small-self views, with the help of all the various teachers who come to us, allows us to proceed with what Snyder calls "the real work."

> The real work is what we really do. And what our lives are. And if we can live the work we have to do, knowing that we are real, and it's real, and that the world is real, then it becomes right. And that's the *real work:* to make the world as real as it is, and to find ourselves as real as we are within it.[7]

The real work, then, is simply what is to be done. It is finding our way in becoming human, in fully engaging the world, in wrestling with all the impossibly gnarly problems that face us on this planet.

For those concerned about such matters, Snyder recommends a combination of clear intention, creative imagination, and good manners. Intention is how you remember you are interested in being awake in the middle of these hard times. Imagination is what he calls "the wild side of consciousness," our small minds at play in Big Mind.[8] Good manners are the root of ethical behavior—not being rude to others (including nature) in thought or deed and not being careless or wasteful. Good manners also include expressions of "please" and "thank you"—and we can extend these to all our actions and relations on the earth. Our teachers can help us learn such manners; the animals and trees would be pleased to see more gracious behavior on our part.

Having confidence in our teachers is a way of building confidence in ourselves. It is a matter of trusting the process, trusting one's self and the world, and looking to the teachers for inspiration. Ultimately though, "teacher" and "student" are just roles we play, not fixed positions or people. Even as we see ourselves as students trying to find a wisdom path to help us, we are also being teachers for others. We are also extending a hand, sharing our experience, building confidence in others so they too can take up the real work of becoming human. The job for both teacher and student is to be willing to show up, to be available for whatever learning might happen. This sort of transmission is happening all the time in daily interactions with colleagues, family members, friends. We need each other, and all the other beings around us, to keep our inspiration charged. We have a long way to go. As Snyder says, "Stay the course, my friends."[9]

The real work is immense and intimate all at once. There are many places to begin. In the next three chapters I take up three fields of green practice that offer multiple opportunities for strengthening our intention. Each of these is crucial to personal and planetary sustainability. We must learn all we can about conserving and maintaining energy effectively. Likewise, we must manage the powerful hooks of desire to understand the penetrating grip of consumerism. And then we must find ways to practice peace as a foundation for sustainability. These fields of practice draw on principles of nonharming, being with the suffering, and engaging the deep view. They test our green commitment and lay out a path for us to follow in taking up the big questions before us.

PART THREE

Acting on Green Values

7

Understanding Energy

"ENERGY" IS A VERY BIG WORD that crosses into many territories of thought. In its myriad forms, it affects everything we do and determines the shape and character of our world. Because energy is instrumental to accomplishing work and to maintaining health, it makes an ideal focus for the green practice path. Human energy use accounts for some of the worst environmental impacts on the planet. We bear a great responsibility to look closely at these impacts and find better alternatives. You do not have to be an expert on green building or hybrid cars to engage the energy conversation. You just need to be willing to observe how energy works and to cultivate healthy social energy relations to sustain you on the green path. This is crucial to being an effective agent in the world, to making wise investments of your energy toward a sustainable planet. In this chapter I introduce ways to develop an awareness of energy as permeating all life activity, and I suggest particular practices for taking up the real work that is to be done with energy.

My own baptism with this subject came unexpectedly in the 1980s when I was working as an environmental science educator for the Point Reyes Bird Observatory in California. Fresh out of grad school, I was enthusiastically engaged in building a brand-new education program complete with bird museum, science interns, teacher training, outside consulting contracts, and a birding travel program. I was learning birds like mad—counting sandpipers at dawn on Bolinas Lagoon, banding songbirds in the afternoons, driving to conferences with other educators, heading off on weekend bird-watching trips. I was a busy young environmentalist! But then things got less rosy. The organization went through a series of stressful leadership transitions, and my health began to unravel. When the director cut my program, I went into a tailspin. Between early hormonal changes and metabolic collapse, I was exhausted. I had almost no energy to do anything. In order to recover from this serious health crash, I had to be very careful not to squander the small amount of energy I had each day. I learned which activities would drain my reserves and which would nourish me. Singing, for example, lifted my heart; talking was a struggle. I took it on as a personal science project. How much could I learn about energy in my own body and in my surroundings?

As part of this project I spent time walking in the coastal landscapes north of San Francisco. At first I could only cover very short distances. So I chose thoughtfully—crashing waves or calm oak trees? Gentle creek or towering redwoods? Each place had its own energy qualities, and these varied by time of day and season. Within each place, individual rocks or trees had their own energetic character. Plants, too, carried different qualities—delicate orchids compared to exuberant sunflowers, graceful willows versus straight trunk pines. I practiced noting and describing these specific energy qualities as a way to pay attention. I watched where I was drawn as a way to understand the state of my own energy. The practice itself became a training, a way of knowing, an introduction to the shape and flow of energy.

DEVELOPING ENERGY AWARENESS

Solar energy, biofuels, green building, acupuncture meridians, yogic chakras—there are more than enough resources available to learn about energy in any of these technical fields. For the green practice path, this level of knowledge is secondary or complementary to a more fundamental awareness of how energy works. For this it is far more useful to be curious than well-informed. I am interested in the basics: how we think about energy, how we perceive energy, and how we respond as energetic beings. You can begin these observations wherever you are; you only need a place to get started. From there, the practice will lead you in the direction of your greatest learning. This approach is not about memorizing facts but rather about developing a kind of energy awareness that can be refined over time. Deepened awareness in one energy arena can inform your awareness of energy in another arena.

Let's begin by thinking about how energy is organized. How does it manifest in nature and in us? And how do we work with energy in our economic system? Energy, in a general sense, takes the form of heat, light, electrical fields, and chemical energy; we can quantify this in ecosystems and human bodies. If you add or subtract energy, things change state—ice to water, water to gas, or living to decomposing. Energy can be thought of as intense and concentrated, for example, as in a very hot forest fire, or diffuse and dispersed, as the heat in the ocean. The ultimate source of energy for all we do is the sun. Solar energy fuels virtually all life processes, though the energy continually changes form. With each transformation, energy is used up, lost or degraded to a more dispersed form. This disorder, or entropy, increases over time, so all physical forms of life tend to come apart, slow down, or become more disorganized. Think, for example, of a forest system where leaves are shed every year, limbs fall with storms, or lightning and wind knock down whole trees, which rot on the forest floor; the place just gets messier every year.

Energy is also constantly being organized into highly complex structures. Sustaining any one of these complex life-forms—for instance, a blue whale or a coral reef—requires a continual supply of energy in the form of nutrients and heat. Sustaining life also requires continual maintenance and care; when energy supplies or upkeep drop off, the result is decline and death. You can bring your attention to the process of energy becoming organized (as in giving birth) or to energy becoming disorganized (as in the act of dying). In reality, things are unraveling and raveling all at the same time. The forest system grows cluttered with downed wood, and then a brush fire races through and creates a charred opening for new growth. A snowstorm leaves everything looking perfect, but then the sun and wind bring blasts of energy and undo the magic.

In Chinese thought, an awareness of energy is central to philosophy and spirituality as well as to understanding the natural world. *Ch'i* can be translated as "matter-energy" or, in a more dynamic sense, "vital force."[1] The Chinese believe that this vital force is imbued with spirit; spirit is not seen as separate from matter as in the usual Western view. The Chinese view of the cosmos is one of continuous transformation and "ceaseless vitality."[2] Nature is this vital energetic force in full display, a dynamic ch'i-filled universe with all beings, including humans, as creative manifestations of matter-energy. When we see all of nature as energy, we intuitively sense our deep relationship with the natural world. As energy beings ourselves, we are part of the all-encompassing universal energy flow; we feel a profound sense of belonging that reflects our true energetic lineage.

To develop awareness of the dynamic, transformative nature of energy, we can focus our attention on patterns and scales of transformation. My colleague Ian Worley studies ice patterns on Lake Champlain from the air. His knowledge of the natural world is informed by hundreds of hours of flying over the landscapes of Vermont and surrounding environs in a small plane. He can tell you if a break in the ice is the result of wind or warming temperatures. He can explain concentric circles on ponds and jagged edges near shore. He knows which parts of the lake freeze first and thaw last and how that reflects water depth, wind disturbance, and solar gain. He has

observed the lake freezing across seasons and years, and he under-
stands all this in the long curve of glacial time when a much bigger
Lake Champlain was solid ice all the way down. Most of us, in contrast, tend to see shorter patterns of time, limited by our own short
life spans. But this bias can be overcome as we develop our awareness of energy dynamics.

The Chinese describe two complementary aspects of ch'i, yin and
yang, which characterize opposite energetic tendencies, for example,
toward motion or stillness, expansion or contraction. "Complementary" is the key word here, since in the West most people are used to
thinking of opposites as exclusionary. The yin-yang symbol expresses
complementarity graphically, with the wholeness of the circle depending on both curving shapes as they fit together. Inside each tear-
drop is a small circle of the opposite color, black in white or white in
black. This indicates that yang energy is never 100 percent yang but
always contains the seeds of yin energy, which will transform the yang
energy into something else. Likewise yin energy is never 100 percent
yin but always carries within it the presence of yang. My husband and
I like to walk along the shore of Lake Champlain to observe moments
of change that reveal this yin-yang dynamic. Early in the season, you
can see clumps of slushy ice congeal into floating lotus leaf-like slabs.
Under the impact of wind or wave action, they disintegrate back into
slush. But if the lake is calm for several days, the lotus forms join together to make a solid sheet out to the breakwater. Later in the season,
after people have walked around on the snow-covered ice, their footprints catch the warming sun and become the first seeds of ice melt.

How do we understand patterns of energy as they are organized
into heating our homes, running our factories, powering our cars? This
is the stuff of coal mines, uranium enrichment, offshore oil drilling,
wind farms, and now cornfields. Energy development requires many
complex steps to create usable forms that human societies can harness
to do work and make our lives comfortable. The ten thousand details of

extraction, production, delivery, and environmental impact are well described in introductory textbooks. To begin developing energy awareness, it is enough to apply the general principles of energy dynamics outlined above. You can look to see where energy is degrading in a system (such as the impact on northern permafrost where oil pipelines cross the tundra) and where energy is being invested in a system (as in government subsidies for oil and gas drilling). We can evaluate sources of commercial energy to see if they generate or destroy vital life force and to what extent. Conventional sources of market energy all inflict significant damage on land and water ecosystems; alternative sources challenge this premise, offering low-impact options such as wind and solar power that harmonize with the natural flows of energy.

We can also look at patterns and scale of energy use and development. Rich countries versus poor, for example—people in the United States and other highly developed countries consume as much energy in one day as the poorest people of the world consume in one year. What keeps such extreme energy inequities in place? We could learn about distribution of coal and oil fields and how these assets determine foreign policy and environmental conflicts. We can observe the debates on conventional versus sustainable energy, and note that right in the middle of the most established lobbies for conventional fuels are the seeds of thinking about renewables. And right in the middle of entrepreneurial start-ups for wind and solar power production are the seeds of corporate thinking and profit-making. We can learn about the energy supplies of our own city or region and practice seeing energy flow as the electrical engineers see it—a complex grid of supply and demand, changing by the minute in relation to weather, season, time of day, local capacity. Any and all of these ways of training your awareness are valuable in understanding and moderating environmental impact due to human energy demands. Some of my students believe that if you spend more time outdoors receiving the energy of the natural world, you will have less need for the industrial energy grid. What do you think?

SOCIAL ENERGY FOR THE GREEN PATH

Developing energy awareness is no small task; it is greatly enhanced by practicing with others on the green path. Buddhists speak of the "three treasures"—the Buddha, or teacher; the dharma, or teachings; and the sangha, or practice community. All three are necessary for spiritual development, perhaps especially the practice community. Working with other people provides encouragement, support, critical mass, and mutual insight. Participating in a practice community reinforces shared ethical guidelines and holds people accountable to their ethical intentions. Yet in a highly individualized society such as the United States, it can be hard to find people willing to commit their time to sharing the green practice path, particularly if it involves something so potentially overwhelming as energy awareness.

The lack of social commitment in the United States was pointed out rather dramatically by sociologist Robert Putnam in his 1995 book, *Bowling Alone,* which showed that American participation in civic and political groups and social activity was in significant decline. He postulated that this trend was the result of the increasing prevalence of leisure technologies for individualized recreation such as television. With the internet, cell phones, and iPods this pattern continues to accelerate. People were choosing freedom to do whatever they wanted, over making commitments to social groups. To counter this trend, a number of cities launched community development projects to build social energy in neighborhoods, supporting sidewalk gardens and farmers markets. Architects redesigned urban business districts to promote interaction and community spirit. Planners promoted smart growth principles to foster citizen participation in local regions.

These days environmental work focuses primarily on building social energy to form effective coalitions. Environmental knowledge in and of itself does not necessarily generate action. More often, peer pressure and contacts between friends are the best means of galvanizing support. As social animals, people need a sense of belonging and the approval of their peers. As environmentalists look more and more toward the work of social psychologists, the individualistic approach to environmental heroism is being replaced by a partnership model, where social relations are built over time to support social transformation.

One of the most effective models I've seen for building social energy for environmental work is that of the Northwest Earth Institute (www.nwei.org), which is now replicated at many state earth institutes around the United States. The institute's founders, Dick and Jean Roy, believed that people needed a simple, non-threatening way to come together and discuss environmental concerns. They began by formulating a short discussion course on the topic of deep ecology and made it available to small groups in churches, companies, and neighborhoods. The NWEI groups met for six weeks to consider the questions raised by their weekly readings and to get to know each other around their points of concern. The first course was a terrific success. NWEI went on to develop six additional courses on voluntary simplicity, sense of place, sustainable living, raising healthy children, climate change, and food, sharing them with groups around the United States. As people found shared interests in the discussion groups, they went on to create youth clubs, weekend project teams, and sustainability committees in their workplaces. Since 1994, these courses have taken place in over nine hundred communities in all fifty states, bringing together over eighty thousand people to generate social energy for the green practice path.

In certain green cities such as Portland, Oregon, or Boulder, Colorado, the social energy for sustainability is so strong that it is shaping city goals. People with strong environmental intentions fill many civic roles in public schools, market systems, food production, transportation, and housing agencies, and even more important, they know each other as friends and colleagues. They work together on their projects and build on their successes; they form a central hub of social energy that reinforces individual commitment to the green practice path. Community members develop best practices and share them with friends and colleagues in other regions; the word spreads. Today in small towns almost anywhere in the United States, you can find some network of people trying to build social energy for the environment. Though their local green practice community may be small, they find ways to gain encouragement and support from those further along on the path.

Some of the most exciting practice partnerships are between far distant points on the globe. With international travel more common and the internet bridging cultures around the world, it is much easier for people to share resources and energy. People on the green path recognize each other across widely divergent cultural traditions and are able to work together for shared environmental goals. Still, it is important to remember that social energy may be organized quite differently from one region to another. Western approaches to building social relations may or may not be appropriate in other settings. Those of us in the industrialized world, for example, rely on electronic technologies to keep our social networks functional. But those modes are not available in many parts of the world. So this is perhaps a cautionary note: building social energy is a complex entropic process that takes time to evolve.

CARETAKING PERSONAL ENERGY

Without well-maintained personal energy, it will be difficult to build social energy for the path. How do we sustain our effort for the long haul without getting discouraged? Is a specific kind of personal energy necessary to take up the green path? I think of John Muir, who could hike for miles on end in the high Sierra with not much more than a scrap of bread for food. I wonder how Rachel Carson kept going even when she was succumbing to breast cancer. How did Thoreau live in that small cabin alone for two years? Maybe all these people were driven by their strong beliefs. Or maybe they were just lucky enough to have unusually strong stamina or determination. I believe it is crucial to study the nature of one's personal energy in order to sustain a commitment to the green practice path. By personal energy I mean how well you use the energy you have and how well you work with its ebbs and flows. Countless environmental activists have hit the wall with severe energy crashes, or "burnout," and have had a difficult time returning to the demands of their work. We must pay attention to this most basic study of energy; we cannot afford to lose time to our own energy crashes.

Some of my own energy insights have come from thinking about the rise and fall of sea energy along the coast. For a long time I clocked my energy by the tides and moon, noting how the energy came up with the rising moon, hit a peak at the full moon, and then turned inward across the waning moon. When I moved from the West Coast to northern Vermont, I began paying more attention to the rise and fall of energy across the year. Here the wide range of climates across the four seasons is a strong determiner of available energy. The summers with their long days bring everyone out to garden and sail and go for long bike rides; the winters with their very short days offer less energy from the sun and take more energy to keep warm. I tend not to begin big projects at the winter solstice when the sun is at a low ebb; I am more productive once the light begins to return.

Yet even within these rhythms there will be days that take a lot of emotional energy—one stress after another, the energy stretched thin. It is not possible to sustain one big emotional day after another; emotions take energy to experience and process. As neurochemical events in the body, each emotion impacts the stability and well-being that nourishes life. Good news and difficult news both take energy to "digest"; for the person following the green path there will be no shortage of either of these. It is important to find a way to steady yourself in the face of continual ups and downs. Some people use meditation or yoga, some use physical exercise, others draw on humor to change their body chemistry and regain equilibrium.

It also takes personal energy to make good environmental choices for yourself, your family, your community, the world. In today's world these do not necessarily come easily. If your energy is low or you are feeling beleaguered, it is hard to be true to your green intentions. If your food or sleep nourishment is erratic, your energy may be unreliable across a day. If you are spiritually discouraged and struggling to contact the bigger wisdom energy of the universe, you may feel alone and isolated in your efforts. It is no small challenge to nurture the green heart and keep your green practices going. You need to maintain daily caretaking habits that can keep your energy steady and efficient. You may also require periodic retreat or vacation or rest to replenish the well. No one can keep going on behalf of the environment day after day without periods for time out and renewal.

Sometimes it can seem like personal caretaking is too self-centered, a secondary priority next to the pressing needs of the environment. Another way to think about it is that you are taking care of yourself on the green path so you can be of service to others. You do your best to manage your personal energy so that it will be available for the hard work that is called for. In my mind, this is central to the green lifeway—understanding that your life can be an offering to others and practicing with that in mind. Working with energy becomes a practice in conservation and efficiency, a personal test of the principles we apply to managing energy flows in the electrical grid. It also becomes a practice in inspiring others to consider green energy choices for themselves. Remembering the laws of entropy and disorder, you can see it takes energy to conserve energy, and it takes energy to organize social and physical systems that will be more energetically sustainable in the long run.

PRACTICING WITH ENERGY

Understanding how energy works makes it possible to apply your effort more effectively on the green practice path. In this section we look at specific practices you can take up as focal points for your effort. Each of these practices can strengthen your energy awareness, both personally and environmentally. They provide entry points for working mindfully with energy at home and in the workplace. As you train your mind and body to "see" energy as it moves in different contexts, you help make energy more transparent, less taken for granted. The more we attend to energy in all its manifestations, the more we will be able to design intelligent life-giving energy systems that are good for both people and the environment.

Mindfulness of Impact

Based on the principle of reducing harm, all the facts point to the need to reduce our energy use because of its impact on the environment. Changing our lightbulbs, buying energy-efficient appliances, insulating our buildings—these are all ways to reduce energy use. But if we are walking the green path, we need a broader framework for our path, a way to practice mindfulness with energy in a wide range of settings. One way to pay attention to energy use is through mapping our energy footprint.

The "footprint" concept was first introduced in an ecological sense by Mathis Wackernagel and William Rees in their 1996 book, *Our Ecological Footprint: Reducing Human Impact on the Earth*. The cover image shows a big fat foot stomping on the globe holding up a city of skyscrapers, houses, electric lines, highways, and factories. The area covered by that foot represents the productive land required to support your consumption and waste disposal. To determine an average ecological footprint, Rees and Wackernagel calculated the per person use of land for energy production, agriculture, water, the built environment, and waste disposal. They then multiplied the number of people in a specific city or region times the average rate of consumption to figure out the total load of that region's population. Not too surprisingly, they found that high-level consumers in the global north had much bigger ecological footprints than modest or minimal consumers in the global south. The typical North American footprint at that time was calculated to be four to five hectares (ten to twelve acres), or about three-plus city blocks. Since then the methodology has been refined substantially, taking many more factors into account. The new figure for the United States is one of the highest on the planet—an astonishing 109 hectares, or 269 acres per person. If everyone on the planet lived the way we do, we would need at least four other planets to support our enormous footprints!

Calculating ecological footprints has now been done for most countries in the world and for many cities. You can fill out a standard internet survey to figure out the size of your personal footprint (see www.ecologicalfootprint.org). As this concept has caught on, people are extending it to think about water footprints, food footprints, and energy footprints. Bringing attention to your energy footprint provides a way to continually evaluate your personal energy use. You can then ask, What increases the size of my energy footprint, and what decreases it? This is the fundamental question in this energy mindfulness practice.

You might note, for example, that energy use tends to go up the more you need to keep a complex situation constant. This pertains to maintaining air temperature in a building or soil moisture in a garden. You might observe where energy leaks out of a system, reducing its effectiveness. Physical energy gets lost through leakage in transport—along gas pipelines or electrical wires; personal energy gets lost in distractions and interruptions. Where energy is bound in objects, it tends to degrade over time—the lawn mower breaks down, the teddy bear loses its stuffing. To develop sources of energy requires inputs of energy, increasing the cumulative energy footprint in turn. Fossil fuels such as oil, gas, and coal that are mined from the ground require extensive infrastructure and environmental mitigation, far more than solar or wind energy development.

Bringing mindfulness to energy flow enables us to evaluate our political and lifestyle choices. We can look closely at what drives our energy use up and wastes energy and then choose alternatives that reduce energy use and husbands valuable energy resources, including our own. What we practice in the microcosm of our homes can help us find better models for energy practices in our communities and regions. Building mindfulness of energy at the local level creates a foundation for sound energy policy at the national level. As more people bring their attention to energy footprints, the level of social awareness will increase to the point of making a cultural paradigm shift possible. This form of mindfulness practice thus has very practical outcomes in both the present moment and the longer curve shift to sustainability. As a practice for the green path, it is grounded in facing the real-world difficulties of peak oil and climate change.

Applying Skillful Action

Energy development, for the most part, is being driven by rapid industrial growth and the prospect of good return on financial investment. If we consider the principles of skillful action in this context, we recall that unskillful actions tend to lead to unhappiness or unhealthiness; skillful actions, by contrast, generate happiness and good health. These are the actions we want for an energy-healthy future. Applying skillful action is a pragmatic way to work with ethical guidelines.

How can a person on the green path take up the practice of skillful action in relation to energy? One place to start is by working with the idea of *efficiency*. We all must consume and use energy to survive; that is part of being a living, breathing organism. But most

of us have drifted a long way from the well-honed energy practices
of our animal ancestry. When you live close to the margin, dealing
with the survival needs of food, shelter, warmth, and safety, every
decision counts. Your energy budget is limited and it must be ex-
pended wisely. In the modern industrial world we have become ac-
customed to profligate use of energy because it is relatively cheap
and easily available. Energy efficiency can be increased by taking
appropriate action to reduce use and review sources of waste in our
homes and workplaces. But individual action alone will not significantly change our overall efficiency. We will need to apply skillful
action to infrastructure changes as well, if we are serious about
reducing our addiction to oil and taking less from the earth. As citizens we must also lobby for energy efficiency in buildings, renewable energy portfolios, and financial incentives for alternative energy
sources.

To take on these challenges in the political and regulatory arena,
we will need to increase energy efficiency in our own lives. One
framework that might be helpful is the economic tool for evaluating
large projects or investments, known as *cost-benefit analysis*. The goal
is to accomplish the most you can using your resources effectively.
Cost-benefit analysis aims for the greatest efficiency in using energy,
labor, and capital as an investment for productivity. This approach
can also apply to the person on the green practice path. You can try
to estimate where your efforts will have the greatest effectiveness and
invest energy there. This usually means building on existing social
network relations and expanding them to include green practices.
In your home, this may mean assessing how your personal space
supports you energetically to be effective. Where have spaces become inaccessible from clutter or dead with disuse? What personal
habits waste your own or others' energy or time (which is another
way to understand energy)? What kinds of backlogs (dishes, bills,
cleaning) keep you from being able to meet your green intentions?
Calculating the costs and benefits of personal habits may make it

easier to simplify your life and thus use your own energy more effi-
ciently.

The Tibetan Buddhist teacher Chögyam Trungpa wrote quite
a bit about energy efficiency; he called it energy "alignment."[3] The
greatest energy loss, he said, comes from inner conflict between body,
heart, and mind. The body wants to do one thing, the heart calls for
another, and the mind tries to mediate between the two. He suggested that spiritual practice could be most helpful in lining up your
intentions to enable you to act effectively and without internal hindrance. Through meditation you can develop the capacity to see and
feel when you are losing energy to internal conflict. This then can be
addressed directly, actions taken, situation resolved, so that body,
heart, and mind can align with full clarity. This clarity, Trungpa felt,
is a powerful force for good in the world. Cultivating energy efficiency
internally can greatly increase your capacity for the tasks of the
green practice path.

ACTING WITH RESTRAINT

Practicing restraint based on moral guidelines means deliberately
choosing to refrain from destructive activities that cause harm. Skillful action in relation to energy efficiency improves the way we use
energy, but we can also choose proactively to use less destructive
energy and less energy overall. Energy conserved from human use
becomes energy available to support life for the rest of the planet. As
people have spread over every region on the globe, our energy needs
have spread with us. Everywhere we drill an oil well, mine for uranium, lay down a gas pipeline, put up a wind turbine, we impact the
lives of the local plants and animals. Choosing not to develop an oil
field or build another big building are acts of restraint, acts of energy
conservation. They are also acts of land and biodiversity conservation

and sometimes also cultural conservation. We can only be proactive in conservation if we find ways to get along with less energy.

One of the most common ethical guidelines across all religions is "do not steal." Behind this admonition is the understanding that social relations cannot function without some degree of stability and trust, and stealing very quickly erodes trust between people. Likewise, environmental relations cannot function if we do not maintain some degree of restraint in our relations. We need to be frank in asking ourselves: does our human energy use entail stealing from the earth? The Hopi and Navajo tribes have spoken out strongly about this, protesting the enormous theft of groundwater from local coal-mining. In northeastern Arizona, Peabody Energy has withdrawn 3.3 million gallons of water per day for thirty-five years, seriously depleting the Navajo aquifer. We must also ask: does our human energy use entail stealing from other people, our fellow earth citizens? Mountaintop removal for coal-mining in West Virginia steals not only the beautiful stream valleys but also the health of the mining families. One black-water spill of liquid waste fouled seventy-five miles of rivers and creeks, polluting drinking water for thousands of residents. Local people have organized to draw attention to the injustice of mountaintop removal. They are clear that this is not an ethical form of mining and want it stopped immediately.

In today's consumer society, all the advertising messages suggest that there is no problem or irritation too big that cannot be solved by a new product. We are encouraged to believe that we can have whatever we want whenever we want it. Restraint is often perceived as some sort of anachronistic throwback to harder times. But especially in today's context, restraint is necessary practice, whether driven by economics or ethics. It is one of the inner disciplines we must take up as part of the green practice path. We simply do not have another four or six or eight planets to exploit. We must curb our appetites before we eat ourselves out of house and home. Holding back from using something up—whether it is a piece of land or your own mental attention—is a way to conserve the energy you value. It is a practice in taking time to pay attention, to say "this matters," to recognize the need to take better care of our important energy resources, in whatever form they may take.

Acting with restraint will sometimes mean "not doing," a form of not stealing from yourself or others. In my own overfull life, I have found "not doing" to be very difficult. The health crash I experienced in my late thirties was a direct result of having almost no comprehension of the verb "to rest." I now understand that resting is a crucial aspect of the green practice path. Sometimes it is necessary to choose to rest in order to conserve your own personal health and the health of your household. Rest time is restorative time, the opportunity for heavily used systems to recover and to integrate the impacts of the day. We can think of health as resiliency, the capacity to respond to illness, disturbance, and stress—in other words, health means having energy available when it is truly needed. Conserving energy is a way to conserve health. Acting with restraint is a way of investing in long-term sustainability. This is the idea behind the practice of observing the Sabbath, which includes the custom of closing shops each week on the day of rest. Each of these are investments in resiliency, a kind of energy savings bank for the future. Such acts of restraint are a practice in stress reduction for both land and people, critical for maintaining strength over the long term for environmental work.

NOW WHAT?

Working with energy can be a lifelong project, one that is particularly appropriate today with the old energy models falling fast. No matter how you approach the conversation, sooner or later you will have to consider the systems drivers that perpetuate our energy patterns. We can personally choose to conserve energy and act with restraint, but meanwhile the market system is actively promoting lifestyles and products that are highly energy intensive. The cheap goods from China that we enjoy are made in factories fueled by coal-fired plants. The more of these goods we buy, the more coal is mined in China to support manufacturing. The engines of trade rely on an endless supply of energy and consumers. In this chapter we have considered developing energy awareness as a central focus on the green practice path. Using energy wisely, not using it when we can, and watching our energy footprint—these tasks will keep the green path clearly in sight. But this alone is not enough. We must look more closely at our own desires for comfort and security to see how these play into the global equation of environmental degradation. Consumerism is fueled by biological need but also by social, psychological, and economic pressures. The more we understand how these work, the less we will be driven by the relentless appetites chewing up the earth. The next chapter opens a conversation on desire and consumption as a second key arena of the green practice path.

8

Working with Desire

THE DESIRE FOR LIFE is the single most hardwired drive we have been given. Every organism thrives according to this desire, investing energy resources to find the necessary requirements for survival. The central message of this desire is: *Look out for me! Look out for me!* Meeting our own personal needs is topmost in our evolutionary instructions; if we fail at this, we die. Because this desire is so core to our well-being, we will do everything we can to make sure we have what we need. Behind this drive is a deep insecurity based on our fragile vulnerability. Our concern for ourselves and our fundamental insecurity play perfectly into the hands of profiteers who exploit our desire, urging us to buy our way to a better life.

Most people would agree that there is more than enough stuff in modern American society. More designer clothes, more cars, more kitchen gadgets, more shop tools, more recreational toys—you name it, we have it! For every piece of stuff, there is a corresponding ecological wake. With some determined sleuthing, you can trace the trail of impacts from raw materials to production and on to distribution and consumer use. It is usually not a pretty sight. But this book is not about the footprints of consumer products; you can find that information in other guides. If we are to take the green practice path seriously, we need to get to the bottom of the whole cycle of consuming. So let's begin with the study of desire.

WHY DESIRE?

Why might it be helpful to work with desire on this practice path? First, it provides a direct and practical route to addressing environmental harm as it is linked to things and services we want. We can study and observe desire in operation at every scale of human society. Families have their desires for the good life; cities and states have theirs as well. Universities, militaries, and prisons all want what they believe will help them thrive and achieve their goals. So does every individual human being. We can begin by observing desire in ourselves; there will be plenty of material here to look at. According to Buddhist teaching, desire is the root of all dissatisfaction. Studying the nature and consequences of desire can illuminate our mostly unconscious choices and their far-reaching consequences.

A second reason to work with desire is serious concern for the stupendous scale of production and consumption in today's global society. More and more of the world's population is expecting to live at the high consumptive rates of industrialized nations. China and India's tremendous economic growth in the last few years is testimony to this goal. Every year the measures of household consumption keep rising, from number of cars and televisions to size of houses. Items once considered luxuries are now seen as necessities. The Worldwatch Institute calculated that the $18 billion spent annually on cosmetics could easily cover estimated global needs for reproductive health care for all women. The almost $14 billion spent on ocean cruises would be enough to provide clean drinking water for everyone in the world.[1] Our priorities seem to be upside down; we invest more in the economic engine of consumerism than in our own well-being.

Third, we use a lot of personal energy trying to satisfy our ever-multiplying desires. In the course of managing the weekly grocery shopping, we must make hundreds of brand decisions and think over and over again, *Will this be satisfying?* Choosing among so many products is an exhausting process, especially if you are trying to buy something unfamiliar. The big box stores don't make it any easier with their mountains of options aisle after weary aisle. We expend precious stores of our life energy or personal ch'i, draining that energy away from other more satisfying activities.

Human desire is not the only driver of global consumption. Increased industrial efficiency and dramatic breakthroughs in computing power are also key drivers. Cheap energy and improved transportation have fueled production and spurred wider marketing of goods. Innovations in extractive technology have made it possible to catch hundreds of tons of fish per day or remove whole mountaintops for coal-mining. Government subsidies, global trade negotiations, and financial incentives such as easy credit have all contributed to skyrocketing rates of consumption. We will keep our focus here on desire because it surfaces everywhere in most of what we do. This is my fourth reason for working with desire on the green practice path: the opportunities are endless. At this moment in history we are in an extremely rich practice field for studying consumer desire.

HOW DOES DESIRE WORK?

You may know the story of young prince Siddhartha, who left his father's palace to seek answers to life's big questions. After living a very protected life, he escaped the palace grounds, only to run into the sobering horrors of illness, aging, and death. The shock of such exposure pulled him away from his royal future, compelling him to find some explanation. With all his being, he wanted to know: *what is the cause of human suffering?* Siddhartha wandered for a number of years, trying all manner of ascetic practices to cultivate spiritual receptivity. His breakthrough moment came after sitting still for a week under a banyan tree, facing every possible form of suffering in his meditation. When he awakened to true understanding, as the sutras say, he was called by Brahma to share his insights with those who would listen. His first teaching, known as the Four Noble Truths, pointed directly to desire as the source of all suffering.

By desire, the Buddha meant grasping or craving after something. The suffering of mental and physical anguish comes from identifying with the craving or the object of the craving. He also spoke of this identification as attachment, what we might call "being hooked." You could think of someone who is hooked on drugs or alcohol as an extreme version of attachment. Craving can be so addicting that it directs all of one's behaviors. This also drives shopaholism, an emerging addiction of the twenty-first century. In many subsequent teachings, the Buddha explained the nature of desire, the causes of desire, the antidotes to desire, and the rewards of detachment from identifying with desire. This is a central theme in early Buddhist texts and potentially a very helpful resource for the green practice path.

The Buddhist teacher Pema Chödrön explains desire using the Tibetan words *shenpa* and *shenlok*.[2] She calls *shenpa* "that sticky feeling" that makes us insecure, tense, wanting to escape our situation. *Shenpa* thrives on our natural uncertainty and discomfort living in a world that is always changing. To get relief from this uneasiness, we look for things that will bring us comfort—food, sex, shopping, perhaps a favorite cappuccino. *Shenpa* is the "urge" for that relief; it can be so strong we sometimes turn to self-destructive things or activities. The key to working with *shenpa* is to recognize it as it comes up. This is more easily said than done; the internal drives to get what we want and avoid what we don't want are very powerful. They arise in the limbic system, often below the level of rational consciousness. We may think we are in charge of our choices, but behind each decision is a lifetime of conditioning. Feeling depressed or upset about environmental concerns can play right into the urge for relief, generating *shenpa* discomfort that is almost unbearable.

The way you break the habitual power of *shenpa* is by choosing not to act on the urge—that is, by refraining from the familiar hooking pattern. Choosing to refrain from action can slow things down enough for you to see what might be going on behind buying that sixth pair of boots you didn't really need. The Tibetan word for refraining or renunciation is *shenlok,* which means to turn *shenpa* upside down, to break open the self-limiting pattern. Meditation can be useful in helping us see how deeply conditioned we are to behave in certain ways. It can show us how we get hooked by marketing messages that stimulate desire and keep us buying an endless stream of products. By refraining from exposure to these messages we open up space for other ways to engage the world besides as a consumer.

Another way to understand desire is through its causes. What is it that keeps the cycle of desire constantly activated and self-reinforcing? While specific causes and conditions for desire are infinite, we can study common patterns that explain the power of the "hooking." One Buddhist teaching on causal origination, known as the Twelve Links, describes the endless chain of desire and its consequences. Each of the twelve links in the cycle is produced by the one that precedes it, and in turn generates the next link. Looking closely at this meta-pattern, we can study the nature of these links and come to some insights about how we consume. This is the first step in breaking the habituated power of the links, providing perhaps a taste of the release the Buddha called "nirvana," or liberation.

Craving or desire does not exist in a vacuum. It is stimulated by feelings that arise in contact with objects in your sense fields. You smell the freshly brewed coffee and almost immediately your mouth and mind send out the strong message: *I want, I want!* Sense feelings can also work in reverse, promoting a sense of aversion. You look in the closet and feel irritated with your outdated wardrobe; the message arises, *Get rid of that stuff!* These feelings are temporary and need to be kept stimulated if a buyer is to give in to the powerful pulls of desire. Thus advertisers and marketers generate a mind-numbing barrage of contact points for the sense organs. Flashing lights, sexy fabrics, big signs, loud music—it quickly adds up to sensory overload.

My friend Bill McKibben once did an experiment of watching every minute of television that aired on a single day on a super-large cable system in Virginia.[3] It more or less took him a whole year to consume and evaluate this much media input. He concluded that one theme stood out above all the others: "*You* are the most important thing on earth." You the television watcher, you the potential consumer who should be taking advantage of the hundreds of advertised products. McKibben cataloged the multiple ways that viewers were bombarded by product advertisements, contrasting this with the completely opposite experience of spending a week in the woods. His experiment revealed just how saturated our media environment is. Today's average consumer in the United States sees more than three thousand ads in the course of a day in every possible venue—from internet pop-ups to sports events, clothing logos to shoe treads. These ads promise a better, happier life, promoting desire for one product after another, all of which eventually fall short.

With your sense consciousnesses already conditioned by advertisements and previous shopping experiences, you are set up to be receptive to even more shopping stimulus. Over time you develop a shopping personality, what the advertisers refer to as "market niche." Despite our personal sense of individual uniqueness, we are captives of our feelings and sense organs in remarkably consistent ways. If we have enjoyed the pleasure from responding to a specific desire, we usually want more of that good feeling. Likewise if we have bad feelings, we want to get rid of them, or at least have less of them. The marketers promise relief from anxiety, fear, and low self-esteem through products. That is the core message ramping up consumerism around the globe: *Have a problem? Fix it with our product!* Never mind any other options such as breathing through that unpleasant feeling, or finding pleasure in non-market experiences. The marketers find it far more profitable to keep us hooked on their products, whatever that takes.

In the Twelve Links model, longer-term patterns of craving result in karmic formations, the more deeply conditioned habits that shape lifetimes and cultures. Western consumer societies have become used to easy access to alcohol, painkillers, pornography, and the abuse that is often associated with such deep conditioning. These karmic patterns can be carried from one generation to the next, transmitting the shape of desire almost below the level of consciousness. We imitate what we see around us; we collectively participate in the endless chasing of desire, believing that temporary relief will satisfy us. The Buddha once said that this chasing was like drinking saltwater. It can never satisfy your thirst and it only leaves you feeling more thirsty.

PRACTICING WITH DESIRE

Motivation for practicing with desire comes easily when you consider the environmental impacts of the objects in your life. Here is where you can really engage systems thinking to support your practice. You can experiment with various levels of refraining to see how hooked you are to your familiar consumer habits. Even though it can be overwhelming to examine things you take for granted, you can take it a step at a time. It is important to be kind to yourself in this process; there is already more than enough finger-wagging going on in our efforts to halt the destruction of the planet. Working with consumerism can be very empowering in developing your green consciousness. None of us is fully aware of how much personal energy we have given over to the our participation in consumer society. It is time to reclaim some of that lost energy and use it more consciously and effectively to support our green practice path.

I'm going to propose four practical methods for working with desire in everyday consumer life. I believe they are broadly applicable and may be helpful with whatever consumer issue is plaguing you at the moment. Some of these methods have been tested for centuries in the crucibles of Buddhist and other monastic traditions. Others are new variations I've tried with students in my "Unlearning Consumerism" course at the University of Vermont. You will likely come up with yet more applications appropriate to your circumstances and consumer concerns. Behind each set of practices is a general principle or approach that is worth studying in itself, just to get to know your tools more intimately.

Paying Full Attention

The first practice is applying mindfulness to common realms of consumerism: buying things, owning things, taking care of things, selling things, giving things. This can be in relationship to food, transportation, energy use, clothing, recreation—anything really. The Buddhist teacher Joseph Goldstein describes mindfulness as "the quality of paying full attention to the moment, opening to the truth of change and impermanence."[4] Mindfulness practice applied to consumption means paying full attention to the act of consuming, the objects of consuming, the feelings of consuming, and the consequences of consuming. For many years Thich Nhat Hanh has offered a simple mindfulness meditation on an orange. He takes a full thirty minutes to lead people through the experience of peeling an orange, separating the segments, holding them in readiness, absorbing the citrus smell, preparing to eat the orange, and finally tasting and chewing the sweet, juicy miracle of orangeness. The lesson is about slowing the consuming process way down to notice its many parts. By being more fully present for the act of consuming, we are more present with our own experience and maybe a little less driven toward the next hook of desire.

You can try this slowing-down process with any sort of consuming. It is especially effective in the terrain of impulse buying. If you do any sort of shopping online, you know how quickly you can act on the impulse to buy. Just a few clicks of the mouse and that good deal on eBay is yours, almost before you thought about it. But if you apply mindfulness to the process, you might notice your body hunched over the computer, your breath suspended in concentration, your fingers moving like speedy little mice on the keyboard. By shifting your attention to direct observation of what is happening, the intoxicating spell of buying is broken, or at least interrupted. That interruption is your golden opportunity to call off the whole purchase, to say to yourself: *wait just a minute—do I really need this?* You have a chance, a microsecond of mindfulness, to ask this question and reconsider.

In my "Unlearning Consumerism" class, the very first assignment is to make a list of everything you own. Everything. The students gasp in terror. Everything? Yes, everything. Clothes, toiletries, kitchen items, books and music, electronics, toys, posters, jewelry, cars, bicycles—everything you are personally responsible for as its owner. This is a crash course in mindfulness of stuff. Taking the time to name everything makes it painfully obvious just exactly how much stuff you have. If you look at each item long enough to notice its existence, you begin to wonder where it all came from, what you are going to do with it, and whether, in fact, it is all really necessary. These are all very helpful questions and worth your attention, even if they make you uncomfortable. We can't begin to really understand the full environmental impact of our things if we don't even know what we have.

But let's bring some mindfulness to the uncomfortable feelings themselves. What comes up? Maybe guilt or shame, perhaps the urge for more, the naked wanting itself. What is that like? Can you bring your attention to notice the wanting itself? Often, it seems, we buy things as a displacement activity to cover over our feelings. The momentary delight of a new thing distracts us from unpleasant feelings we'd rather not acknowledge. But most likely it is these very feelings that most want your full attention. Giving them that attention may reduce the need to consume and thus also reduce your impact on the earth. Once you consider what it really means to consume, you can begin to see how your own consuming is part of a vast human appetite gnawing away at the planet. It is important to truly see this, to fully observe the cumulative impact of so much consuming.

Engaging the Links

Insight on this scale can be quite galvanizing; you want to take action, to do something, to somehow improve the situation. Mindfulness practice stimulates motivation, so let's look at a second method for working with desire: actively confronting the links of craving. Recall how desire is stimulated by feeling states generated by the senses (including, in the Buddhist view, the mental sixth sense of thought). One way to counteract the seemingly automatic body responses to sensory and feeling information is through rational thought. Using the cerebral cortex offers an alternative to the evolutionary hardwiring of the reptile brain. By actively using logic, knowledge, and critical thinking, you can challenge the power of these co-dependent links of desire.

For my class I've designed a couple of easy cerebral cortex exercises that provide some quick information in relation to food choices. The first is the Food Energy Log. You make a list of everything you have eaten for three days, with the ingredients separated out as best you can—that is, not "sandwich" but "cheese, tomato, lettuce, bread," and so forth. Next to the list of ingredients you make five columns for your ratings. For each food, you assign a 0, 1, 2, or 3 for three aspects of the food (as best you can estimate): (a) the amount of packaging, (b) the distance shipped, and (c) the energy used in harvest and production. In the fourth column you double the harvest and production energy number, since this factor contributes the greatest environmental impact. Then add up (a) + (b) + (d) to get a score of 0–12 for each food. The numbers, imprecise as they are, still reveal certain trends. A locally grown, unpackaged apple, for example, might receive a 2, indicating its relatively low energy impact. In contrast, a cup of coffee made from beans shipped from Ethiopia might receive a 12, with high ratings in all three categories. Our rough class data across the years indicates the high energy foods are meat products and beverages—tea from China, hot chocolate from Ghana, orange juice from Florida. You can work with consumer desire by deciding to make it a priority to reduce your food energy footprint. To do this, you would try to reduce the high-impact foods in your diet and increase the low-impact foods. Very quickly you can see what your own consumption patterns tell you about desire and energy.

Another thing you can do is read the labels on food products. This can tell you something about how far the product has traveled and how complex the production process is. The idea is to counter the habitual responses to desire by informing yourself about the actual things you are consuming. With the rapid expansion in the food market for green products, you need to look closely at product claims to check for greenwashing hype. Some green labels such as "fair trade" or "organic" provide useful certified information about the product. Other labels, such as "natural," "eco-safe," or "biodegradable" only make general claims that have not been verified by a third party. You can check over a hundred green product labels at www.greener choices.org/eco-labels/ to give you some ballast against the powerful pull of green marketing strategies.

If your curiosity is aroused by either of these exercises, you can research individual products and learn their stories. You need to be prepared to change your diet though; once you know how something is produced, you may have to reconsider what you eat. In the last few years there has been a surge of resources to help track such stories, and they are quite illuminating. I started with *Stuff: The Secret Lives of Everyday Things,* a great little book with ten chapters on common items—shoes, T-shirts, aluminum cans, and so on. The World-watch Institute has now come out with an online guide, *The Good Stuff? A Behind-the-Scenes Guide to the Things We Buy* (www.worldwatch.org/taxonomy/term/44). If you want in-depth journalistic reporting, take a look at *Fast Food Nation* by Eric Schlosser or *The Omnivore's Dilemma* by Michael Pollan. The market research shows that as consumers become more informed about their choices, they want green alternatives. By working with desire through rational analysis, you can strengthen your environmental intentions, sending a message to producers that "green counts."

Reviewing Consumer Habits

If you take up the study of desire, you will sooner or later be curious to try some experiments in restraint. Refraining or taking a break from familiar patterns can open up space for reviewing your consumer habits. Contemplative retreats are especially good for this, the longer the better. Some teachers suggest setting aside "mindfulness days," once a month or maybe even once a week, to settle the mind. Weekend programs at retreat centers offer periods of silence and calming practices that can act as antidotes to the runaway impulses of desire. Even if the focus of the retreat is not unlearning consumerism, it can still be a welcome relief to be in a setting that doesn't reinforce the wanting. To enable people to slow down and be more present, retreat centers generally stick to simplified activity schedules, simple meals, and minimal social distraction.

One of the more elaborate training practices during Zen retreats is serving and eating meals *oriyoki* style. Every choreographed step of this Japanese meal form is meant to highlight the practice of "just enough." Meals are held in silence in the meditation hall, with experienced servers, pots in hand, briskly traveling the long rows of meditators. With a simple hand gesture, you indicate how much you want, the same for second servings. The meal is served in three bowls for breakfast and lunch, two for dinner. To begin the meal, you carefully unwrap your stacked bowls, lay out the small tablecloth, and arrange the chopsticks, spoon, napkin, and scraper in their designated spots. During service and eating, you have endless opportunity to observe the mind's relationship to food. When you have eaten "just enough," and everyone else is done, the servers come around with hot washing water in teakettles. With another simple gesture, you indicate how much water you want, and then you scrape and wipe your bowls until they are clean—usually with less than half a cup of water. Then back they go into their wrapping, like a Japanese gift, waiting for you when the next meal comes around. The whole process is remarkably efficient, offering many ways to minimize desire and reduce waste. For some people, *oriyoki* is a hallmark of Zen precision, but I see it as a beautifully crafted green dance, kind to eaters and eaten alike.

Going on retreat can help cultivate your motivation for the green practice path and for whatever environmental work you choose to take up. We may think our idealistic intentions are clear or solid, but they are usually much more ambiguous than we realize. On retreat you have the chance to be more honest about your own mixed motivations and see where you are vulnerable to consumer messages playing on your inner conflicts. You can notice your favorite addictions or attachments and how you organize yourself to sustain them. Sitting still for a period, or taking the time to walk quietly in a natural setting, can help you clarify what matters most to you. It is a wonderful gift to be able to see with minimal interruption or distraction. You can hold your intention in focus, feeling it resonate in your mind and heart, and then consciously choose to set your intention on your top priorities. This gift to yourself can then be carried back into everyday life to support you in your home and work practice.

Inevitably we think, *Oh, it's better on retreat!* or, *Oh, it's better at home!"* Tasting the simpler life can be enticing, but still we must return to our complicated lives full of desire. A useful principle for negotiating this territory is what Buddhists call the Middle Way. Not too hot, not too cold; not too luxurious, not too spare. Green zealots can sometimes insist on one extreme or another, but mostly these positions are not very sustainable. The Middle Way is about balance, moderation, and continuous reflection on what is appropriate. There is no single equation for what is right at any given time. Continuous reflection is key, for conditions and options are changing constantly. What seems to be good for the environment at one point in time may later turn out to be problematic. What you are able to commit to as a young person may not be possible in a different phase of your life. Attachments change; so do desires. As we consider ways to simplify, it is important to cultivate a sense of contentment that can inform our Middle Way choices of moderation. This is the fourth practical approach I want to offer in working with desire.

Choosing Well-Being

Contentment is an underrated state of mind in consumer cultures. We hardly know how to recognize it or what to do when we feel content. Maybe we think it's boring. Or maybe the cynic inside us doesn't believe it really exists. In Buddhist philosophy, contentment is highly valued as a state free of desire. When you are content, you are actually okay with everything just as it is. In that moment you are not struggling with any complaints or dissatisfactions. You are fully present to yourself and the world around you. A relaxed body, a calm mind, a sense of well-being—nothing more is needed. Can you recognize this state? You realize you don't need to go to the store to get anything; you have enough. You don't need to be entertained by sensory stimulus; you have enough. You don't need to fill a gaping hole of hunger, anger, loneliness, or exhaustion; you are okay just as you are. This is quite a powerful teaching for combating the endless marketing of dissatisfaction.

But how do you arrive at contentment? For that, I can offer no simple recipe. However, you might gain some insight from trying a "technology fast." This is another of my student experiments, based on age-old practices of renunciation. Thai Buddhist monks, for example, eat only at daybreak and noon, giving up their evening meal. Trappist monks give up talking and communicate silently in their cloistered halls. Giving up something you rely on, even if only temporarily, is a way to see what it means to you and how it shapes your thoughts and behaviors. Some people try giving up meat, some people refrain from alcohol. In a technology fast, you abstain from using an everyday technology that you normally rely on in some aspect of your life. This could be a car, a cell phone, a laptop computer, the television, the dishwasher, or, for something more challenging, try giving up electricity! One of my students did all her homework by candlelight and the glow of her battery-powered laptop for three days as her technology fast. Three days seems to be long enough to taste life without your chosen technology; one day might be too easy, a week might make it difficult to keep your job and household together. Removing the impact of the television, or whatever technology you choose, opens up new possibilities for contentment through doing without.

An opposite experiment is not to give something up but to completely enjoy and appreciate it. Here the idea is to fully inhabit the material world and realize how fortunate most of us are to be so well-supported in our basic needs. So often our minds are off in the clouds somewhere, hardly noticing the many remarkable things that enrich our lives. If you try to take up this practice in a general sort of way, it doesn't really work; you need to have a focus for the practice. Here's one: knives. Knives are sharp, hazardous, very useful, and good ones are beautifully crafted. In Zen kitchens, students are trained in what is called "knife practice," that is, how to take care of knives properly. First, this means noticing the properties of the knife while you are using it—its weight, its sharp edge, the way it feels in your hand, how it cuts. Then, when you're done with the knife, it means washing and drying it immediately and putting it back in the chopping block to keep the knife safe. Doing this practice faithfully changes your relationship with knives. You are practicing caretaking as an investment in the well-being of things. This is the opposite of consuming things until they are gone.

Practicing contentment opens up the whole conversation about well-being and quality of life. We know now that more stuff does not necessarily equate to more happiness. In study after study, psychologists have shown that well-being is associated with good health, satisfying work, supportive relationships, and a sense of internal control in your life. These are exactly the things that are under assault in our fast-paced consumer lifestyles. If we want to choose well-being as our aim on this planet, we can design communities, food systems, and modes of transportation that promote well-being. We can replace infrastructures of consumption with infrastructures of well-being.[5] We can develop indicators of contentment that help point us in a direction of sustainability rather than endless desire. We don't have to keep consuming the planet like ravenous hungry ghosts hooked on craving. We can choose another path based on well-being, on true care for the material world, and on using "just enough" for each of us.

When we choose a life of well-being and contentment, we find that we are cultivating peace, which is the third arena for green path practice discussed in the next chapter. Contentment rests on inner peace and is supported by social stability and well-being. It takes effort and intention to create opportunities for contentment and peace. Choosing peace reframes the way we relate to the earth and its inhabitants. Choosing peace helps to calm the fires of desire and the conflicts they generate. This is how we practice non-harming as a complement to our work with energy and desire. Peacemaking is an act of love and an investment of personal energy in a more stable world. We create hope for sustainability through creating the conditions for peace. The gift of this work calls forth the much-needed efforts of those on the green practice path.

9

Practicing Peace

IMAGINE THIS SCENE: a sea of people as far as the eye can see, all sitting silently, peacefully, filling the temple grounds for a very special ceremony. It is March 15, 2002 in war-torn Sri Lanka, and the celebration is Peace Samadhi Day, one of the largest meditations for peace in world history.[1] The event has been organized by Sarvodaya Shramadana, a grassroots movement based on Mahatma Gandhi's principles of self-reliance. Founded in 1958, Sarvodaya has a long-standing commitment to peace advocacy, with outreach programs in fifteen thousand villages. The purpose of the event is linking up villages from each side of the conflict to rebuild each others' homes and temples. Within each village a local team has been coordinating daily, weekly, and monthly mass-meditation programs in preparation for the big event. Sarvodaya's founder, Dr. A. T. Ariyaratne, called for the mass meditation to change the country's "psychosphere" and deepen people's desire to bring an end to war.

In another scene closer to home, a circle of people meditate quietly in a threatened grove of coast redwoods in California, adding a calm presence to the trees with their soft breathing. They are holding the peace in a tense showdown between corporate timber executives and citizen tree protectors. The people in this circle are

ACTING ON GREEN VALUES

modern ecosattvas, dedicated to protecting life and easing environmental suffering. The old-growth giants are hundreds of years old;
their wood brings a handsome profit in the global market. The struggle over these trees is a conflict in values of major proportion with
no obvious resolution in sight. Like Sri Ariyaratne, the California
demonstrators hope to change the psychosphere of the conflict surrounding the redwoods by bringing attention to the remarkable gift
of the trees.

These stories strike me as both inspirational and extraordinary,
touchstones for the imagination in taking up the practice of peace on
the green path. Peace is a complicated term, overlain with idealistic
hope, conflicting agendas, and challenging diplomacy. Approaches
to peace vary from spiritual to political, global to personal. Peace and
the environment are not often addressed in the same conversations.
Peace activists typically focus on different priorities than do environmental activists. Peace negotiators deal with different laws and
customs than environmental problem solvers. Yet both share the
goals of stability and support for healthy human and environmental
systems.

Working toward peace is congruent with the principles described
in the first two chapters of this book—reducing harm and being with
the suffering. I believe that peace work is an important focus for the
green practice path, providing a necessary complement to working
with energy and desire. As with these two other practice arenas, the
opportunities are endless and the work is both internal and external.
The more you learn about peacemaking in yourself, the more helpful you can be in offering that knowledge to others dealing with
environmental conflict. The more experience you gain in reducing
harm to the earth, the less harm you will inflict on yourself.

Anger has not always been the most effective tool in addressing
environmental abuse. It quickly turns to self-righteousness, and sides
become polarized in self-defense. Moral outrage is certainly justified
as a response to the terrible decimations of whole ecosystems and

the many beautiful creatures within them. How can so much killing be acceptable? How can we not fight back? And yet anger itself is exhausting; it generates so much stress on the body and mind. In the aftermath of anger comes discouragement, depression, helplessness—a weary frustration that nothing can be made right. These states of mind are the territory of peacemaking, the motivation for learning how to find a well of calm that can sustain you on the green path when you encounter conflict and violence.

PEACE, CONFLICT, AND ENVIRONMENT

The turn into the twenty-first century marked a number of shifts in global politics and economics, with significantly heightened emphasis on security of all kinds—national security, food security, climate security. Behind these concerns lie very real insecurities that human beings will not be able to get enough of what we need to survive. If we look at conflict around the world today, it can often be linked to increasing concern for securing necessary resources such as oil. The long struggle in Iraq is centered in an oil-rich zone; Nigeria, Burma, and Chechnya, to name just a few others, have also suffered violence over oil development and production.

In his book *Resource Wars,* peace studies scholar Michael Klare describes three key features of such resource conflicts today. First, there is an escalating demand worldwide for raw materials of all kinds as the global population continues to rise. With more people, there is more need for shelter, food, energy, and water. This demand is further accelerated by increasing rates of consumption, already high in developed countries and growing steadily in developing countries, especially India and China. Add to this the spread of industrialization, and the soaring production of goods creates a seemingly insatiable demand for resources. Second, we are, in fact, running out of some things. Fisheries, forests, and fossil fuels are all in decline, and certain minerals have become so rare as to be quite costly. A number of studies estimate we are near peak oil availability, and water supplies are in significant shortage in many places around the earth. Third, many key resources lie in contested border areas or offshore economic zones, raising the potential for dispute between nations. Upstream states take the water they need to the aggravation of downstream states. Already we are seeing contests over who will get the mineral resources made accessible by the melting of the Arctic ice sheet. Klare's point is that all these stressors present new sources of competition, friction, and conflict. And each factor tends to reinforce the destabilizing aspects of the others.

While many resource conflicts are resolved through diplomacy and negotiation, some unravel to the point of violence and war. War, from whatever causes, always takes a toll on the environment. In Cambodia, agricultural fields still lie fallow because of the density of leftover land mines. In Vietnam, bomb-sized craters have become mosquito breeding grounds, carrying disease into war-damaged areas. Militaries and their leaders have chosen scorched-earth policies as part of their war tactics in Iraq and Colombia, destroying forest cover or crop fields by bombs or chemical spraying. Militaries themselves are some of the biggest users of resources, especially oil. A single B-52 bomber uses over three thousand gallons of fuel in a single hour; worldwide, nearly one quarter of all jet fuel is used by the military.[2] Lands damaged by war take time to heal; long-lasting insults may alter land productivity permanently. The soils of Iraq, for example, will be contaminated with depleted uranium of used ammunition for a very long time.

Recognizing the costly environmental impacts of conflict, some are suggesting the alternative: using the environment in a peacemaking role. When two conflicting parties view their environmental problems in isolation, they often ignore the complex ecosystem relationships that cross their borders. Japan, for instance, is downwind of China's acres and acres of air-polluting factories. Addressing environmental issues can build peaceful relations, because these discussions require a long-term perspective and local engagement in the peacemaking process. Through the process of building political relations that are less polarizing, it is possible to transform conflict into cooperation.

Environmental peacemaking initiatives to date aim either to prevent conflict or create a sustainable mechanism for peace. Many conflicts arise from challenges over local resource use or misuse as well as inadequate capacity at the institutional level. The most direct form of environmental peacemaking may be preventative, taking action to build capacity and relieve resource pressures before conflict arises. In conflicts where a specific environmental challenge has been identified as a contributing cause, the peace-building process can focus on shared environmental goals. Even where governments are locked in a history of hostile relations, they are sometimes willing to have dialogue around maintaining their life-support systems. In certain entrenched situations such as the dry region of Israel and Palestine, the management of water resources is a necessary condition for sustainable peace. If water needs and allocation mechanisms are not resolved, disputes will continue.

Some of the most hopeful initiatives in transboundary conservation are the creation of peace parks such as Waterton-Glacier International Peace Park on the U.S.-Canadian border. Established in 1932, Waterton is seen as a model for peace and cooperation; similar parks are being proposed for the Kashmir border area between India and Pakistan as well as in West Africa and Indochina. In the Kuril Islands, long disputed between Japan and Russia, the beautiful red-crowned crane and other endangered species would gain much-needed protection from the creation of an international peace park. Such efforts at environmental peacekeeping have surged since the beginning of the twenty-first century. As of 2005 over 818 countries have become involved in 188 initiatives for environmental peace. This is, indeed, a promising sign, though many negotiations are still in progress.

DEFINING PEACE

"Peace," like "energy," is one of those words that sets off a chain of associations in the mind, and these can vary tremendously from one context to another. The original meaning of *pacem* or *pax,* the Latin word for peace, is an agreement achieved by contract or agreement. In this sense, it means that the conflict is resolved and the parties have agreed to certain rules or behaviors they will abide by in order to maintain the peace. These days such agreements pertain to whole nations and regions, making peace agreements more complex than ever. Peace treaties run for many pages and often take years of diplomacy before agreements are reached.

In his thoughtful collection of essays, *Peace: Research, Eduction, Action* (1975), the Norwegian peace scholar Johan Galtung suggests several concepts that may be useful in looking at environmental peacemaking. He defines "negative peace" as the absence of violence between groups and "positive peace" as proactive cooperation and efforts toward social justice. If we apply these terms to environmental peace relations, "negative" or benign peace would be the absence of violence toward ecosystems, landscapes, plants, and animals. "Positive" peace would be marked by efforts toward sustainability and a commitment to just and respectful relations with other beings. Examples of "benign peace" might be wildlife refuges or protected areas with limited human access. Proactive peace might be seen in the efforts of organic farmers to promote healthy soils and agricultural ecosystems.

We can also look at the distinction between direct violence and structural violence, which are the opposite of peace. Clear-cutting, acid rain, bottom trawling, and damming of rivers all cause direct violence to the earth. Trees, fish, lakes, rivers, and the ten thousand beings that dwell in, on, and around them are killed, crippled, and starved by these actions. Extreme violence such as the decimation of centuries-old cedars and redwoods could be likened to a holocaust, a scale of violence of frightening and awesome proportions. This is painful to think about; it is devastating to witness. Structural violence is less obvious, though the effects may be even more widespread. Economic policies, infrastructure, and trade can encourage erosion of ecosystem stability. Freeways may encroach on cougar habitat to improve transport. Soybean fields are replacing rainforests to fulfill biofuel development strategies. Migratory bird wetlands degrade from sewage treatment-plant runoff. Much of the structural violence that affects earth systems may not have been intended, but in many cases, little thought has been given to its prevention either.

Some political scientists have tried to define peace in terms of environmental security, extending the deep concern for national security that has marked the recent fear-based policies of the United States. "Security" derives from the Latin word *securus,* meaning "without sorrow or worries." Environmental security redefines security to focus on environmental threats to planetary well-being. Advocates for the concept point out the obvious link between ecosystem degradation and nation-state health. But some of these conversations have generated concern that environmental protection could become militarized, and this approach would further reinforce the reigning paradigm of human domination over the earth. Poor countries tend to view environmental security as a "rich country" agenda, a way to protect and sequester natural resources for the use of those wealthy or powerful enough to enforce this agenda. Casting environmental problems in security terms may block more cooperative approaches based in peacekeeping.

Understanding peace work from an environmental perspective means building on the extensive peace-building efforts that are already under way in many parts of the world. Such efforts are no longer solely the domain of national diplomats. International finance institutions such as the World Bank and the International Monetary

Fund are key players in determining economic packages that can either mitigate or increase environmental destruction. Small-arms traders and private militaries also carry strong influence in shaping the nature of local conflicts. Global military spending is one of the most lucrative businesses on the planet right now, exceeding $1.2 trillion in 2006. The United States leads the world in weapons spending, accounting for 46 percent of this total. The United States is the top supplier of global arms, providing 63 percent of small arms to nations involved in conflict or defense.[3]

Non-state actors also play important roles in conflict resolution and peace-building. Among these are 60,000 major transnational corporations (TNCs), such as Shell Oil and Coca Cola; 5,800 international non-governmental organizations (INGOs), such as Amnesty International and the Nature Conservancy; 10,000 nationally based NGOs, some with considerable international influence; and, not least of all, 250 intergovernmental organizations including the United Nations.[4] From an environmental peacekeeping perspective, this shift of influence is good news. Pressure can be placed on TNCs to withdraw from "conflict trade" in lucrative resources such as diamonds and timber that finance wars. INGOs and NGOs can work together to support alternative peacekeeping models and bring local players to the table. Citizens in distant states can offer support to these efforts through the organizational campaigns of the NGOs. Often the role of NGOs has been to provide humanitarian assistance for people caught in the cross-fires of the conflicts. But increasingly, environmental groups are stepping in to protect indigenous tribes and their lands as well as the ecosystems under assault in war zones.

PERSONAL PEACE PRACTICE

Practicing peace as part of the green path can take many forms. As with the practices of understanding energy and working with desire, the opportunities are endless, arising continuously in all manner of contexts. If you offer this practice your full intention you will find that peacemaking and peacekeeping are part of what we do every day to support stability in our lives. We cannot function well under conditions of chaos and conflict; some measure of peace and equilibrium is necessary for life to flourish. But it is remarkable how much of our life energy is spent in sparring with ourselves or others, or being fearful of attack, or cleaning up the aftermath of conflict. Working toward peace is something we cultivate with persistent effort, learning our way into the practice. Peace with others, peace with the earth, peace within our hearts—each of these can reinforce our motivation to keep peacemaking at the center of the green practice path.

We can approach the practice of peace in a systematic way, observing our own behaviors and thoughts as we deepen our attention to peacemaking. I find it helpful to think in terms of body, speech, and mind as major arenas of effort. Peace work with the body is a form of caretaking of the most intimate environment we inhabit, our own flesh and blood. Each person has their own triggers of conflict, their own expressions of resistance. It is important to honor the history of your own experience and how that experience has been recorded in the memory cells of the body. You might try making a map of your own conflict history to see what it can tell you. Contemplative practices can increase awareness of internal fighting or defense reactions and also entrain new patterns that calm the body. Tai chi and yoga, for example, can literally change your neural and hormonal flow patterns. Meditation and prayer also calm the body through stillness and centering. As these forms of peace-building become familiar in the social landscape, more environmentalists are coming to see the long-term benefits of contemplative body practice.

Engrained speech habits also benefit from committing to peace work. Environmentalists, unfortunately, have a reputation for self-righteous blaming and poor listening. We seem to be so anxious to be heard that we are impatient with hearing others' perspectives. It is too easy to lash out at the parties responsible for causing environmental suffering. "Right speech" is one of the spokes in the wheel of the Buddhist Eightfold Path. It means not lying, not gossiping, not slandering, and not putting others down to puff yourself up. It means not participating in oppressive speech that silences others' voices. Practicing right speech is a practice in humility, a real effort to remember that your words are only one point of view. Harsh or thoughtless words so easily derail the peacemaking process. This is very sobering. The slow cultivation of cooperative relationships is a fragile thing that thrives best on kind speech.

Peace-building in the mind is perhaps the most challenging practice in terms of peace work. We believe our thoughts are invisible to others because we think them within the privacy of our own minds. But thoughts guide speech and behavior, reflecting a lifetime of conditioning that we only partially understand. Fighting thoughts displace peace-building thoughts because they so quickly mobilize the attack-and-defend system. If you are working to save something that matters dearly to you, you may be using fighting thoughts to keep yourself energized. But fighting thoughts need enemies to blame and wrongs to be righted. It can be pretty limiting and draining to rely on fighting thoughts for momentum. I am recommending peace-building practice for the mind as a long-term investment in an approach that is ultimately more sustainable.

It has taken me some time to come to this conclusion. I grew up in a culture of argument; whatever the issue, everyone in my family wanted to prove they were right, and others were therefore wrong. We did not seem to be able to have a reasonable discussion with different points of view. Our household was characterized by constant competition for power based on who could win the most arguments. Family order, personality, and gender dynamics all played into this, but no matter how much my mother tried to teach us about social justice, we persisted in our put-downs. These constant battles drove me out into the woods behind our house where I sought silence and refuge. The trees, the beautiful yogis of the forest, became my teachers of peace practice.

Turning to nature as practice partner comes easily for many on the green path. If you find pleasure in hiking, camping, canoeing, or any of the many ways of being in nature, you likely have had some moments of profound peace outside. The big sky bright with stars, the full moon rising in the clouds, the deep quiet of snow in the woods. We receive these gifts and they help us remember that peace exists; it is part of our world already. (This is not to say that nature is always calm; we know that storms come, tempests blow, trees fall and crack into a million splinters.) And peace in nature is found not only in wild areas. Walking by the fields on the edge of town or quietly appreciating the backyard tree—these, too, are portals to peace practice.

Meditation teachers encourage us to find this place of peace in ourselves through conscious breathing. When we are upset or filled with conflict, our ch'i is flying everywhere, looking for something to hit or running to get out of a situation. If we stop for a moment and concentrate on our breathing, we bring our awareness back to the body and return home. If the anger cannot be calmed in a few breaths, we can try walking meditation, aligning the breath with our steps, letting the earth support us. These simple breathing practices are very grounding. They stop the conflict from escalating; they allow us to be present with ourselves and to find a touchstone of reassurance in the solid ground. Maha Ghosananda, sometimes called the Gandhi of Cambodia, explained that "making peace must be done every day. It is like walking. You have to make every step. If you forget a step, then you fall down . . . If we protect the world, we protect ourselves. If we harm the world, we harm ourselves. We are in the same boat. Therefore, we must take care of the boat."[5]

MUTUAL LIVING TOGETHER

Peace studies scholars in Japan have written extensively about living together peacefully, something they call *kyosei*. This word was first introduced in the field of biology to describe symbiosis in plants and animals. But it has been taken up by the social sciences and by philosophers to address more generally the conditions for peaceful coexistence. One of the early models of *kyosei* was based on toleration, in which social groups maintain their own cultural values and traditions and respectfully recognize those of other social groups. This model was critiqued for being too separatist and oriented mostly toward keeping Japanese values intact and protected from outside influence. A more recent model of *kyosei* interprets living together as a conversation where parties enter into a common forum of conviviality. The idea is simply to enjoy the natural play of agreement, disagreement, controversy, and competition in everyday interaction of society. A third model takes this concept even further to achieve commonly shared goals such as ecological sustainability and social justice. The Japanese speak of *kyosei* between humanity and the natural environment, imagining peaceful coexistence filled with dynamic exchange. In Japan, *kyosei* as a word is much in vogue and is being used widely to reframe values discussions in many contexts, from academic disciplines to environmental planning.[6]

The international peace negotiator William Ury has written extensively about the peacemaking process as a careful dance between sides. In his book *Getting to Peace* (1999), he recommends the role of a "third side"; this is a party outside the immediate conflict but with a vested interest in a peaceful outcome. The third-side party can clarify differences, provide protection to threatened parties, and educate where knowledge is needed. Someone with green path sensibilities can draw on the practices suggested in earlier chapters of this book to help stabilize conflict or cultivate convivial living together.

Ury describes ten roles, all of which apply to environmental situations. Three of these roles are particularly well-suited for the green practice path.

The first is the *bridge builder,* who works to prevent conflict by strengthening fragile relations in the human and ecological web. This strengthening might be accomplished through regulatory agreements or round-table discussions that bring people together to find mutually workable solutions to environmental problems. The third-side party can help facilitate understanding across divergent points of view. Where conflicts have escalated and relations are damaged, a green path practitioner might be drawn to the role of *healer.* A third side party with a commitment to peacekeeping and compassionate action can be a valuable asset in moving a situation forward to resolution. You can use your skills in relational thinking to analyze the causes and conditions of the conflict and work to heal brokenness and damage. The role of healer may take considerable diplomacy and patience depending on the degree of injury. The healer helps conflicting parties understand each others' positions and find a better solution to the problems at hand.

Where environmental conflict has become entrenched and resolution is not in sight, taking a third-side peacekeeping role requires more courage. The massive gold-mining operations in Indonesia, for example, are firmly protected by the national military to squelch local conflict. The history of assault on the land and people in that context is so deeply ingrained that it will not be easy to resolve. Healing is not possible until the injury-making stops. Here a green path practitioner might serve in the role of *witness,* making the public aware of what is happening to plants and animals under attack. Bringing others' attention to the problem exposes harmful behavior, which can then generate public pressure for change. Rather than polarizing an already tense situation further, the witness acts with respect toward all parties, bearing witness without accusation, reporting facts without condemnation.

Whatever your role in environmental peacekeeping, it is crucial to think of yourself as an active agent in Indra's Net. What you do really matters. Maha Ghosananda spoke of this as broadcasting mental waves of peace from your personal radio station. If we have peaceful mental waves, then they go out beyond us, touching the hearts of other beings. Thich Nhat Hanh suggests that we plant seeds of joy and peace. You don't know exactly how and when they will sprout, but you water them with your hope and kindness and take good care of them when they manifest as peaceful activity in the world. Every moment we have the opportunity to broadcast waves of peace. Every moment we can choose to plant seeds of joy. Intention is very important in this practice. In the ancient tradition of *gathas,* or meditation poems, Zen teacher Robert Aitken expresses his intention in this way:

> Hearing the crickets at night
> I vow with all beings
> to find my place in the harmony
> crickets enjoy with the stars.[7]

If you recite such a vow of intention each day, you will deepen your commitment to peacemaking and gain strength for the challenges on the green practice path.

Important seeds of peace were planted in the first efforts to write an international Earth Charter. With remarkable courage and determination, Mikhail Gorbachev and a team of representatives from countries around the world sat down to craft a list of principles that could guide the world in caring for the earth. It was an ambitious undertaking. The charter went through draft after draft, a ten-year conversation that exposed and reflected many diverse perspectives, not always reconcilable. But the committee members stayed with the process, struggling over appropriate concepts and wording, thinking always of how to sustain the earth for all life. The final version of the Earth Charter recognizes peace and justice as necessary for ecological well-being. It urges citizens of the world to

- promote a culture of tolerance, nonviolence, and peace
- encourage and support mutual understanding, solidarity, and cooperation among all peoples and within and among nations
- implement comprehensive strategies to prevent violent conflict and use collaborative problem-solving to manage and resolve environmental conflicts.[8]

In early September 2001, the year before the charter was brought to the United Nations for approval, we held a day of festivities in northern Vermont to celebrate its completion. Over a thousand people gathered at Shelburne Farms, walking in silence across the hills as one body flowing peacefully together. The inspiring words of the charter were written on colorful banners and strung along the entry path. We sang, we listened, we danced together in the spirit of *kyosei* and the Earth Charter. Children and artists from all over the state brought handmade books of prayers for the earth, each one full of heart and genuine desire for peace. One by one they were placed in a large wooden ark, beautifully handcrafted and painted for the journey. The prayers were blessed by all the big and small people who came together that day. Eventually all those seeds of peace made their way to the United Nations, where thousands of people saw the children's books and read their prayers. It was a moving testimony for the charter's own call for the way forward on our mutual green path:

Let ours be a time remembered for the awakening of a new reverence for life, the firm resolve to achieve sustainability, the quickening of the struggle for justice and peace, and the joyful celebration of life.[9]

Desire for peace in our hearts and peace with all beings is a compelling call. I believe this call is bringing many people to the green practice path. The work we are engaged in is hard work, but it is real work; it is the work that is to be done. Practicing together we can help each other through the difficulties and give thanks for the moments of contentment. And most of all, we can pass the green spark on, so there will be others following in our footsteps. This is not an impossible vision; it is our journey to well-being.

Notes

Chapter 1. Reducing Harm

1. Michael Brower and Warren Leon, *The Consumer's Guide to Effective Environmental Choices* (New York: Three Rivers Press, 1999).
2. Thich Nhat Hanh, *For a Future to be Possible: Commentaries on the Five Wonderful Precepts* (Berkeley: Parallax Press, 1993), 132.
3. *For a Future to be Possible*, 13.
4. Daniel Leighton, *Bodhisattva Archetypes: Classic Buddhist Guides to Awakening and their Modern Expression* (New York: Penguin Arkana, 1998), 1.

Chapter 2. Being with the Suffering

1. Elizabeth Roberts and Elias Amidon, eds., *Earth Prayers* (San Francisco: Harpers, 1991), 146.
2. Thich Nhat Hanh, *For a Future to be Possible: Commentaries on the Five Wonderful Precepts* (Berkeley: Parallax Press, 1993), 132.
3. Bhante Henepola Gunaratana, *Eight Mindful Steps to Happiness* (Boston: Wisdom Publications, 2001).

Chapter 3. Embracing the Deep View

1. Joanna Macy and Molly Brown Young, *Coming Back to Life: Practices to Reconnect Our Lives, Our World* (Gabriola Island, British Columbia: New Society Publishers, 1998), 119–21.
2. Ludwig von Bertalanffy, *General System Theory: Foundations, Development, Applications* (New York: G. Braziller, 1969).
3. Chung-Ying Cheng, "On the Environmental Ethics of the Tao and the Ch'i," in *Worldviews, Religion, and the Environment: A Global Anthology,* ed. Richard C. Foltz (Belmont, Calif.: Wadsworth, 2003), 224.

4. Gregory Bateson, *Steps to an Ecology of Mind: Collected Essays in Anthropology, Psychiatry, Evolution, and Epistemology* (Chicago: University of Chicago Press, 1972).

5. Mitchell Thomashow, *Ecological Identity: Becoming a Reflective Environmentalist* (Cambridge, Mass.: MIT Press, 1995); and Thich Nhat Hanh, *Being Peace* (Berkeley, Calif.: Parallax Press, 1987), 87.

6. Rachel Carson, *The Edge of the Sea,* (Cambridge, Mass.: Riverside Press, 1955), 249.

7. Thich Nhat Hanh, "The Sun My Heart," in *Dharma Rain: Sources of Buddhist Environmentalism,* ed. Stephanie Kaza and Kenneth Kraft (Boston: Shambhala Publications, 2000), 89.

8. Eihei Dōgen, "Time-Being," in *Moon in a Dewdrop,* trans. Kazuaki Tanahashi (San Francisco: North Point Press, 1985), 77.

Chapter 4. Entering the Stream

1. Daniel Leighton, *Bodhisattva Archetypes: Classic Buddhist Guides to Awakening and their Modern Expression* (New York: Penguin Arkana, 1998), 162.

2. John A. Grim, "Native North American Worldviews and Ecology," in *Worldviews and Ecology,* ed. Mary Evelyn Tucker and John Grim (Lewisburg, Penn.: Bucknell University Press, 1993), 42.

Chapter 5. Engaging Skillful Effort

1. Joanna Macy and Molly Brown Young, *Coming Back to Life: Practices to Reconnect Our Lives, Our World* (Gabriola Island, British Columbia: New Society Publishers, 1998).

2. Ibid., 190.

3. Bhante Henepola Gunaratana, *Eight Mindful Steps to Happiness* (Boston: Wisdom Publications, 2001), 161–86.

Chapter 6. Seeking Wisdom Sources

1. Summarized in Steven C. Rockefeller, "The Wisdom of Reverence for Life," in *The Greening of Faith: God, the Environment, and the Good Life,* ed. John E. Carroll, Paul Brockelman, and Mary Westfall (Hanover, N.H.: University Press of New England, 1997), 44–61.

2. Arne Naess, "The Shallow and the Deep, Long-Range Ecological Movement, *Inquiry* 16 (Spring 1973).

3. John Seed, Joanna Macy, Pat Fleming, and Arne Naess, *Thinking Like a Mountain: Towards a Council of All Beings* (Philadelphia, Penn: New Society Publishers, 1988).

4. Aldo Leopold, "Thinking Like a Mountain," in *A Sand County Almanac: Outdoor Reflections and Essays* (New York: Oxford University Press, 1966), 129–133.

5. Rita Gross, *Soaring and Settling: Six Buddhist Perspectives on Contemporary Social and Religious Issues* (New York: Continuum, 1998), 184.

6. Gary Snyder, *The Practice of the Wild* (San Francisco: North Point Press, 1990), 150.

7. Gary Snyder, *The Real Work: Interviews and Talks, 1964–1979,* ed. William Scott McLean (New York: New Directions, 1980), 82.

8. Gary Snyder, *Back on the Fire* (Emeryville, Calif.: Shoemaker and Hoard, 2007), 44.
9. Ibid., 25.

Chapter 7. Understanding Energy

1. Tu Weiming, "The Continuity of Being: Chinese Visions of Nature," in *Worldviews, Religion, and the Environment: A Global Anthology,* ed. Richard C. Foltz, (Belmont, Calif.: Wadsworth, 2003), 210.
2. Ibid., 211.
3. Chögyam Trungpa, *Shambhala: The Sacred Path of the Warrior* (New York: Bantam, 1986), 85–88.

Chapter 8. Working with Desire

1. Brian Halwell and Lisa Mastny, eds., *State of the World 2004* (New York: W.W. Norton, 2004),10.
2. Pema Chödrön, "How We Get Hooked, How We Get Unhooked," *Shambhala Sun* (March 2003).
3. Bill McKibben, *The Age of Missing Information* (New York: Plume, 1993).
4. Joseph Goldstein, "Desire, Delusion, and DVDs" in Stephanie Kaza, ed. *Hooked! Buddhist Writings on Greed, Desire, and the Urge to Consume* (Boston: Shambhala Publications, 2005) 17–26.
5. Gary Gardner and Erick Assadourian, "Rethinking the Good Life," in Brian Halwell and Lisa Mastny, eds. *State of the World 2004,* ed. Brian Halwell and Lisa Mastny (New York: W.W. Norton, 2004), 164–79.

Chapter 9. Practicing Peace

1. For more information on Sarvodaya mass meditations, see www.sarvodaya.org.
2. Michael Renner, "Assessing the Military's War on the Environment," in *State of the World 1991* (New York: W.W. Norton, 1991), 137.
3. Jennifer Wedekind, "A World of Weapons," in *Multinational Monitor* (May/June 2007), 5.
4. Alex J. Bellamy, Paul Williams, and Stuart Griffin; *Understanding Peacekeeping* (Cambridge, UK: Polity Press, 2004), 19.
5. Scott A. Hunt, ed., *The Future of Peace: On the Front Lines with the World's Great Peacemakers* (San Francisco: HarperSanFrancisco, 2002), 282, 284.
6. Yoichiro Murakami, Noriko Kawamura, and Shin Ciba; *Toward a Peacable Future: Redefining Peace, Security, and Kyosei from a Multidisciplinary Perspective* (Pullman, Wash.: Thomas S. Foley Institute for Public Policy and Public Service, 2005), xiv–xv.
7. Robert Aitken, *The Dragon Who Never Sleeps* (Monterey, Ky.: Larkspur Press, 1990), 39.
8. The Earth Charter text is available at www.earthcharter.org.
9. Ibid.

Further Resources

A guide to sources or topics mentioned in the text. There are many other very fine resources in print and on the web available for your extended explorations.

Chapter 1. Reducing Harm

Brower, Michael, and Leon Warren. *The Consumer's Guide to Effective Environmental Choices.* New York: Three Rivers Press, 1999.

Kingsolver, Barbara. *Animal, Vegetable, Miracle: A Year of Food Life.* New York: Harper-Collins, 2007.

Leighton, Taigen Daniel. *Bodhisattva Archetypes: Classic Buddhist Guides to Awakening and their Modern Expression.* New York: Penguin Arkana, 1998.

McKibben, Bill. *Deep Economy: The Wealth of Communities and the Durable Future.* New York: Times Books, 2007.

Nabhan, Gary. *Coming Home to Eat: The Pleasures and Politics of Local Foods.* New York: W.W. Norton, 2002.

Pollan, Michael. *The Omnivore's Dilemma: A Natural History of Four Meals.* New York: Penguin, 2006.

Schlosser, Eric. *Fast Food Nation: The Dark Side of the All-American Meal.* Boston: Houghton Mifflin, 2001.

Singer, Peter. *Animal Liberation.* New York: Avon Books, 1977.

Snyder, Gary. "Nets of Beads, Webs of Cells" in *A Place in Space.* San Francisco: North Point Press, 1995, 65-73,

Websites

Center for Whole Communities: www.wholecommunities.org
Thich Nhat Hanh: www.plumvillage.org
Union of Concerned Scientists: www.ucsusa.org

Chapter 2. Being with the Suffering

Grossman, Elizabeth. *High Tech Trash.* Washington, D.C.: Island Press, 2006.

Guha, Ramachandra. *Environmentalism: A Global History.* New York: Longman, 2000.

Gunaratana, Bhante Henepola. *Eight Mindful Steps to Happiness.* Boston: Wisdom Publications, 2001.

McDaniel, Jay. "Red Grace and Green Grace." In *With Roots and Wings: Christianity in an Age of Ecology and Dialogue.* Maryknoll, N.Y.: Orbis Books, 1995, 42–58.

Roberts, J. Timmons, and Parks, Bradley C. *A Climate of Injustice: Global Inequality, North-South Politics, and Climate Policy.* Cambridge, Mass.: MIT Press, 2007.

Smith, Ted; Sonnenfeld, David A.; and Pellow, David Naguib, eds. *Challenging the Chip: Labor Rights and Environmental Justice in the Global Electronics Industry.* Philadelphia: Temple University Press, 2006.

Websites

Electronic waste: www.ban.org

Mountaintop removal: www.mountainjusticesummer.org/facts/steps.php

Pacific Ocean plastics: www.algalita.org/pelagic_plastic.html

Chapter 3. Embracing the Deep View

Bateson, Gregory. *Steps to an Ecology of Mind: Collected Essays in Anthropology, Psychiatry, Evolution, and Epistemology.* Chicago: University of Chicago Press, 1972.

Cook, Francis. *Hua-yen Buddhism: The Jewel Net of Indra.* University Park: Pennsylvania State University Press, 1977.

Lewis, Thomas; Amini, Fari; and Lannon, Richard. *A General Theory of Love.* New York: Random House, 2000.

Thomashow, Mitchell. *Ecological Identity: Becoming a Reflective Environmentalist.* Cambridge, Mass.: MIT Press, 1995.

Websites

Deep Time: http://bcn.boulder.co.us/basin/local/sustain2.html

Genesis Farm, Miriam MacGillis: www.genesisfarm.org

Chapter 4. Entering the Stream

Hawken, Paul. *Blessed Unrest: How the Largest Movement in the World Came into Being and Why No One Saw It Coming.* New York: Penguin, 2007.

Lear, Linda. *Rachel Carson: Witness for Nature.* New York: Henry Holt and Company, 1997.

Lerner, Steve. *Eco-pioneers: Practical Visionaries Solving Today's Environmental Problems.* Cambridge, Mass.: MIT Press, 1997.

Macy, Joanna. *Widening Circles: A Memoir.* Gabriola Island, British Columbia: New Society Publishers, 2000.

McLeod, Melvin. *Mindful Politics: A Buddhist Guide to Making the World a Better Place.* Somerville, Mass.: Wisdom Publications, 2006.
Meine, Curt. *Aldo Leopold: His Life and Work.* Madison, Wis.: University of Wisconsin Press, 1988.

Websites

An Inconvenient Truth: www.climatecrisis.net
Green Sanctuary movement: http://uuministryforearth.org/grs_overview.htm
Teal Farm: www.tealfarm.com
World Index of Social and Environmental Responsibility: www.wiserearth.org

Chapter 5. Engaging Skillful Effort

Guenther, Herbert V. and Kawamura, Leslie S., trans. *Mind in Buddhist Psychology.* Emeryville, Calif.: Dharma Publishing, 1975.
Gunaratana, Bhante Henepola. *Eight Mindful Steps to Happiness.* Boston: Wisdom Publications, 2001.
His Holiness the Dalai Lama. *Ethics for the New Millenium.* New York: Riverhead Books, 1999.
Kalupahana, David. *Principles of Buddhist Psychology.* Albany, N.Y.: State University of New York Press, 1987.
Macy, Joanna, and Young, Molly Brown. *Coming Back to Life: Practices to Reconnect Our Lives, Our World.* Gabriola Island, British Columbia: New Society Publishers, 1998.

Websites

H. H. the Dalai Lama: www.dalailama.com
Joanna Macy: www.joannamacy.net

Chapter 6. Seeking Wisdom Sources

Devall, Bill and Sessions, George. *Deep Ecology.* Salt Lake City, Utah: G.M. Smith, 1985.
Hill, Julia Butterfly. *The Legacy of Luna: The Story of a Tree, a Woman, and the Struggle to Save the Redwoods.* New York: HarperSanFrancisco, 2000.
Kaza, Stephanie. *The Attentive Heart: Conversations with Trees.* New York: Ballantine Books, 1993.
Loori, John Daido. *Teachings of the Earth: Zen and the Environment.* Boston: Shambhala Publications, 2007.
Schweitzer, Albert. *Out of My Life and Thought: An Autobiography.* Translated by C. T. Campion. New York: H. Holt and company, 1933.
Seed, John; Macy, Joanna; Fleming, Pat; Naess, Arne. *Thinking Like a Mountain: Towards a Council of All Beings.* Philadelphia: New Society Publishers, 1988.
Snyder, Gary. *The Real Work: Interviews and Talks, 1964-1979.* William Scott McLean. New York: New Directions, 1980.
Williams, Terry Tempest. *Refuge: An Unnatural History of Family and Place.* New York: Vintage Books, 1992.

Websites

Ecology Hall of Fame: www.ecotopia.org/ehof/index.html

Chapter 7. Understanding Energy

Putnam, Robert D. *Bowling Alone: The Collapse and Revival of American Community.* New York: Simon & Schuster, 2000.

Trungpa, Chögyam. *Shambhala: The Sacred Path of the Warrior.* New York: Bantam, 1986.

Wackernagel, Mathis, and Rees, William. *Our Ecological Footprint: Reducing Human Impact on the Earth.* Gabriola, British Columbia: New Society Publishers, 1996.

Websites

Carbon calculator: www.epa.gov/climatechange/emissions/ind_calculator.html
Co-op America: www.coopamerica.org
Ecological footprint quiz: http://www.footprintnetwork.org
Interfaith Power and Light: www.theregenerationproject.org
Northwest Earth Institute: www.nwei.org
Union of Concerned Scientists: www.ucsusa.org/clean_energy

Chapter 8. Working with Desire

Durning, Alan. *How Much Is Enough? The Consumer Society and the Future of the Earth.* New York: W.W. Norton, 1992.

Halwell, Brian, and Mastny, Lisa, eds. *State of the World 2004.* New York: W.W. Norton, 2004.

Hunt-Badiner, Allan, *Mindfulness in the Marketplace: Compassionate Responses to Consumerism.* Berkeley, Calif.: Parallax Press, 2002.

Kaza, Stephanie, ed. *Hooked! Buddhist Writings on Greed, Desire, and the Urge to Consume.* Boston: Shambhala Publications, 2005.

McKibben, Bill. *The Age of Missing Information.* New York: Plume, 1993.

Merkel, Jim. *Radical Simplicity: Small Footprints on a Finite Earth.* Gabriola Island, British Columbia: New Society Publishers, 2003.

Ryan, John C., and Durning, Alan Thein. *Stuff: The Secret Lives of Everyday Things.* Seattle: Northwest Environment Watch, 1997.

Websites

Center for a New American Dream: www.newdream.org
Community of Mindful Living: www.iamhome.org/about.htm
Eco-labels: www.greenerchoices.org/eco-labels
The Good Stuff: www.worldwatch.org

Chapter 9. Practicing Peace

Ali, Saleem H., ed. *Peace Parks: Conservation and Conflict Resolution.* Cambridge, Mass.: MIT Press, 2007.

Galtung, Johan. *Peace: Research, Education, Action.* Copenhagen: Christian Ejlers, 1975.

Klare, Michael T. *Resource Wars: The New Landscape of Global Conflict.* New York: Metropolitan Books, 2001.

Rosenberg, Marshall B. *Nonviolent Communication: A Language of Life.* Encinitas, CA: PuddleDancer Press, 2003.

Ury, William. *Getting to Peace.* New York: Viking, 1999.

Websites

The Earth Charter: www.earthcharter.org

Sarvodaya Shramadana: www.sarvodaya.org

Worldwide military spending: www.sipri.org/contents/webmaster/databases